JOB
GENERATION

JOB GENERATION

PUTTING AMERICA BACK TO WORK...AGAIN!

STEVEN R. MUSICK

Advantage®

Published by Advantage, Charleston, South Carolina.
Member of Advantage Media Group.

ADVANTAGE is a registered trademark and the Advantage colophon is a trademark of Advantage Media Group, Inc.

Printed in the United States of America.

ISBN: 978-1-59932-388-6
LCCN: 2013941921

This publication is designed to provide accurate and authoritative information in regard to the subject matter covered. It is sold with the understanding that the publisher is not engaged in rendering legal, accounting, or other professional services. If legal advice or other expert assistance is required, the services of a competent professional person should be sought.

Advantage Media Group is proud to be a part of the Tree Neutral® program. Tree Neutral offsets the number of trees consumed in the production and printing of this book by taking proactive steps such as planting trees in direct proportion to the number of trees used to print books. To learn more about Tree Neutral, please visit **www.treeneutral.com**. To learn more about Advantage's commitment to being a responsible steward of the environment, please visit **www.advantagefamily.com/green**

Advantage Media Group is a publisher of business, self-improvement, and professional development books and online learning. We help entrepreneurs, business leaders, and professionals share their Stories, Passion, and Knowledge to help others Learn & Grow. Do you have a manuscript or book idea that you would like us to consider for publishing? Please visit **advantagefamily.com** or call **1.866.775.1696**.

This book is dedicated to the lioness of a woman I met in 1975 and married in 1978 and who is the only reason I am still alive in 2013. She took in a social dwarf when no one else would. Together we built lives of immeasurable depth and richness. Elaine J. Musick is a world-class lady.

Table of Contents

9 | Acknowledgments

11 | Foreword by Wes Roberts

15 | Introduction: *Why Write This Kind of Book?*

21 | Chapter 1: *How to Read This Book*

25 | Chapter 2: *Entrepreneurial Element One: Creativity and the Big Idea*

37 | Chapter 3: *Entrepreneurial Element Two: Who Benefits and by How Much?*

45 | Chapter 4: *Entrepreneurial Element Three: Fantastic People*

61 | Chapter 5: *Entrepreneurial Element Four: Laser Beam Focus*

71 | **Chapter 6:** *Entrepreneurial Element Five:*
Capital Formation

85 | **Chapter 7:** *Entrepreneurial Element Six:*
Coordinated Orchestration

97 | **Chapter 8:** *It Actually Does Take a Hero*

109 | **Chapter 9:** *Success Measures*

117 | **Chapter 10:** *The Next Megatrend in*
American Business

131 | Curriculum

137 | Appendix

155 | About the Author

157 | What's in the Musick Library?

Acknowledgments

The following people in this section are part of a decanting process. They have poured into me and encouraged me to pour into others. In this way, the liquid the world desperately needs continues to be recycled, expanding with each measure of pouring.

My thanks to Wes and Judy Roberts—keep your springs flowing; to my family at home, Elaine, Jarrod, Steph, Brett, Amy, Aaron, and Sarah; to my work family who get more of the waking me than my home family—some of them are singed around the edges from overexposure; to Pat, Judd, Mabel, Jarrod, Julia, Judy, Erin, La Rae, and Ken; to my colleagues at the University of Denver, especially Ilene and George; to my students who have taught me more than they have learned from me, the mentor, especially Holi and Ania, who paved the way for hundreds of others; and to the clients mentioned in these pages, and the others not mentioned but who nonetheless were an integral part of the shaping of me and of our firm, Destiny Capital.

Finally, my thanks to the entire team at Advantage Media. The idea for this work began in June 2012. Advantage was the only publisher who would work with me, an entrepreneurial leader with limited writing skills. You have made a silk purse from a sow's ear. None of this would have occurred without your involvement.

Foreword
by Wes Roberts

Back in the days of my own undergraduate work, way back in the '60s, I had the good fortune to meet up with one of the most significant mentors of my life. His creative brilliance unnerved me, challenged me, pushed me into new places I'd not been internally or externally, and dared to suggest that there was more to my being on Planet Earth than I could currently imagine.

I will be forever grateful.

As will you, reading this material. You have your own hopes and dreams that keep grabbing your imagination. You are mature enough to recognize that this life is not all about you. You are beginning to realize that you (yes, you!) can make a difference in our world, even as you gain the courage to create new avenues of commerce and care.

> Logic will get you from A to Z; imagination will get you everywhere.
>
> **—ALBERT EINSTEIN**

What you read, study, ponder, dream about, and do with what you will read here, no matter your age, gender, ethnicity, or life experience, is about to take you on a ride that *will* change your life. Fortunately, Steve Musick has lived and is committed to living what he teaches. All his students, clients and coworkers will tell you he's the "real deal!" What he shares here has been lived out in countless lives around the globe.

If you want to build a ship, don't drum up the men to gather wood, divide the work, and give orders. Instead, teach them to yearn for the vast and endless sea.

—ANTOINE DE SAINT-EXUPÉRY

Too often we look for the magic pill that will make us successful, the quick fix that will make us known, the fast track to fame and fortune. Few I know are against success, being known, even fame and fortune. Any and/or all of that may be in your future. However, those are outcomes that may bless the moment, but are not the first goals to pursue.

The Job Generation is going to help you gain a better way of thinking about your work in your own future. You will be encouraged to take leaps of faith that will bring fulfillment that your inner self longs for. If you absorb what is suggested here, your life will change in time.

Through the trial-and-error bumps and bruises of making it across the finish lines of your own dreams, if you dare to absorb what is suggested here, you will be set free to soar into your own future in a manner that will both affirm your purpose on the planet and add your own unique stamp to the needed common good of our world.

This takes work. Good work. Hard work. The wisdom here will encourage you to move forward to the success you hope to live out all your days.

Back in the early '60s, while in college, it was my good fortune to have a 30-minute conversation with the man who is quoted above. I had the profound privilege of getting a summer job at Disneyland. For a lad raised in rural Oregon, this was amazing then and still is today. That quote by Walt (at Disneyland all people, except for Mr. Toad, go by their first names) has become the legendary mantra of the whole Disney enterprise. He also spoke it to me on that day.

> If you can dream it,
> you can do it.
>
> **—WALT DISNEY**

What Steve will guide you through here is equally powerful. His clients affirm that. You will too, in time, as you grow the businesses germinating in your own creative soul.

Though I live in Colorado, I conclude this foreword in a hotel room in downtown Los Angeles, California. Dawn is breaking on the massive buildings. The sounds of a city coming alive are capturing my attention. I will be participating in a conference of 900+ world-changing entrepreneurs, the vast majority, half my age. It is these men and women who give me hope for our future in both large and small endeavors.

> Don't die without
> fulfilling your purpose.
>
> **—JAACHYNMA N. E. AGU,**
> *THE PRINCE AND THE PAUPER*

You too bring me hope, though we will most likely never meet. Glean from this creative wisdom. Make it your own. Change your world, right where you are. Mentor others to do the same. Ahead of time I congratulate you on your hard-earned successes because you took to heart and lived well what my good friend and colleague Steve Musick is suggesting here.

Wes Roberts

LEADERSHIP MENTOR/ORGANIZATIONAL DESIGNER
Leadership Design Group: The School of Mentoring, Mentoring w/o Borders, Three3rds Media, Parker, Colorado

Introduction
Why Write This Kind of Book?

Strong emotion is a powerful motivator and this book is part of an explosion of emotion.

The firing pin struck the little brass dot on the shell, setting it all in motion, in June 2012 at a commencement address for the University of Denver, where I am now employed as an adjunct professor of entrepreneurial leadership.

Listening to this keynote address for the commencement was a hinge point in my life, a point at which a strong course correction took place. The message delivered by the keynote speaker was about inheriting a paradise from his father's generation.

Reflecting back, he spoke of leaving a mess, a significant mess of debt in particular, as his legacy for the next generation of workers.

The following is quoted directly from his speech: "We broke it. Now it's your job to fix it."

Clip, snap, ping, bang.

An explosion went off inside of me at those words. I remember General Colin Powell said, "If you broke it, you bought it." That was his statement about the Iraq War. Screaming within me was an absolute "No!" It's not the job of the incoming grads to fix what my generation broke. It's *my* responsibility.

I am married to a lioness of a woman. She is someone who, in my decades of marriage to her, always points out to me the things I know I should be doing. After a month of my having percolated just below the boiling point on this broke-it-fix-it line of thinking, she glanced up over her newspaper at breakfast one morning that summer and purred gently, "How long are you going to just sit over there and stew about this?"

I started to answer in an "Excuse me, what in the world can I do?" manner. Her gentle purring question turned into a steely-eyed glare. The lioness part of her character was about to pounce, as usual, for my benefit.

"You!" she said. "Yes, you can do something about this. You are perfectly positioned to speak to this job generation problem."

The teeth bared. The claws unsheathed. She came forth full-force, putting her newspaper down to emphasize the point. "Who else has 37 years of entrepreneurial experience?" she asked. "Who else is descended from trappers and traders and mountain men having entrepreneurism in their DNA? Who else has three master's degrees in management and financial services and international economics? Who else has ten years of working with college students at a private university dedicated to the public good? You've been agitated too deep and for too long since that commencement speech. This thing goes all the way to your soul. When are you going to respond?"

And, as usual, she was right.

The first step I took was to reorganize my company, Destiny Capital, an entrepreneurial leader in financial management and consulting, freeing up some of my time to work on a solution. I wrote this manuscript, which was accepted with lightning speed in just a few weeks by the editor-in-chief of the publishing house—a miraculous feat, I have come to realize.

Most importantly, to truly give back to the generations coming after me, I applied to the Daniels College of Business in the Management Department of the University of Denver to teach, as an adjunct professor, on the subject of entrepreneurial leadership. My course is designed to enlighten and ignite students who are entrepreneurially setting themselves up on a trajectory to charter a business enterprise. I introduce my students to others who are experts in the area, bringing entrepreneurial leadership from concept to reality.

> **My classes are also a training ground for students who want to work in entrepreneurial organizations."**

My classes are also a training ground for students who want to work in entrepreneurial organizations. I am an entrepreneur with my own self-started company, and interestingly, my application to the university was my first professional job application. I began teaching there in 2013. The material we learn and discuss there—the textbook for the class—is the source of this book.

My publisher, Advantage, plugged me into the university's national network to be a public speaker. I speak on two topics. The first, "Mirror Time," is a message to existing entrepreneurial leaders. It is essentially a fireside conversation. You see, many entrepreneurs are very focused, busy people – often too busy. In "Mirror Time" we sequester business leaders, leading them into conversations they could have with themselves but don't take the time on their own. The second topic is "Job Generation," which is a presentation to workers who have not been able to secure the right job in America. I build upon my ten years of experience in mentoring students at the University of Denver prior to teaching this class of my own.

We are going to do what we can to fix what we broke.

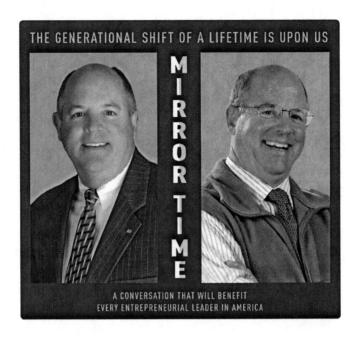

THE GENERATIONAL SHIFT OF A LIFETIME IS UPON US

MIRROR TIME

A CONVERSATION THAT WILL BENEFIT
EVERY ENTREPRENEURIAL LEADER IN AMERICA

Putting America back to work again is the theme of my class, my work, and this book. The focus is on new entrepreneurial companies and small and intermediate entrepreneurial organizations generating jobs for the next era of American business.

Why You Should Read Job Generation

As an entrepreneurial leader, this book will help you revitalize your enterprise and prepare to harness the next megatrend in America.

If you are an unsecured worker seeking employment, this book will outline where the jobs are going to be and how to position yourself to stand out in a crowd.

Welcome aboard for this job-generating journey!

CHAPTER 1

How to Read This Book

A chapter telling you how to read a book? Yes. And why would you need that? Because you paid to hold this book in your hands, and you are investing your time in these pages. Yet you paid for only two-thirds of a book.

Did I just lose you with my reference to two-thirds of a book? Every word, all the illustrations, each story told—each is unfinished. This is an abridged literary work.

The Musick library in my home is large and diverse. A friend of mine was over the other day, and seeing a book in the library's business and economics section, he asked, "Hey, you've got the latest Thomas Friedman. Can I borrow it?"

"Sure. It's a library after all," I said. He snatched the book, sliding it right into his backpack. I was grinning to myself.

Sure enough, two days later he called and said, "It's impossible to read that book I borrowed. You underlined it. You highlighted. You wrote all over in the white spaces and in the margins. Sheesh!"

I replied that Thomas Friedman simply started the book. I made it mine by finishing it. His initial work was the first two-thirds, and it sparked my mind into action. My highlights, my underlining, my notes, all of my thought processes involved in absorbing his words completed the work.

> **"You are invited, actually encouraged, to make this book yours."**

And so it is here. This book in your hands now is printed in an oversized format to allow you to insert your own notes. You are invited, actually encouraged, to make this book yours. Highlight it. Write in it. Make notes from beginning to end, right in its pages. Please finish it.

Each chapter has an Applications and Takeaways section at the end. The material has direct relevance to two main groups. One is designated "EL" and is written specifically for entrepreneurial leaders. The second is designated "UW" for unsecured workers. These are essentially the Cliff Notes versions of the entire chapter. They are designed to exercise and ignite your gray matter. You actually may want to read the end of the chapters first and then flip back to the beginning and read with an activated mind.

As a college professor, I've discovered that learning occurs best in a relaxed environment. Moreover, as an experienced financial adviser, I also know that probing, deep, emotional subjects such as money are best conducted in a place of safety. As I said, you invested in this book and are likely going to invest another several hours of time and thought to read it—perhaps another hour and a half to mark it all up. My expectation is that the time you invest with this book could be life changing.

Deep discussions about the world of work are what I call a "womb-room" experience. I invite you to look more closely at Chapter 2 of this book for a deeper understanding of my concept of a Womb Room, a place of contemplation where ideas are born.

And right now, I am going to give you an unusual guarantee. If this investment in your time and most of your money was an outright bust, please notify us. See Chapter 10 for all of our contact information. Tell us why it was a waste of your time and monetary investment. We will refund your purchase price. Your feedback—both positive and negative—will help with the second edition of *Jobs Generation*.

> "My expectation is that the time you invest with this book could be life changing."

This work in your hands is one of continuous improvement and reflects a permanent-student mentality. It's been a 37-year practice of Destiny Capital, my organization, to refund fees to dissatisfied clients. The guarantee on the book is an extension of that principle.

Enjoy your read.

CHAPTER 2

Entrepreneurial Element One: Creativity and the Big Idea

Years ago, I was in the Los Angeles area with a dead weekend in between two conferences. I have a friend who's also a client—his name's McNair Wilson—and who also happened to be attending the second conference. Wanting to have some fun personal time before the conference, I contacted him.

We arranged to meet for a late breakfast at the Grand Californian Hotel. When I saw him in the lobby, he threw his arms out wide and exclaimed loudly, "Welcome to my hotel!"

After a big army hug, we got seated, and I gave him a cocker-spaniel tilt of the head and said, "Your hotel? Did you win the lottery and not tell me?" I mean, seriously, would Disney allow a private citizen to just belly-up and buy one of their properties? The place where we were sitting was inside Disney's California Adventure theme park in Anaheim.

McNair Wilson spent a decade working for Disney, most of it as an imagineer, one of Disney's development and design team. The best day of his life was when Disney hired him. The second best day of his life was when his boss, Marty Sklar, called him into his office and said, "McNair, we need to release you because, frankly, we're holding you back. Here's a severance check and some contacts to help you get your individual, independent business started."

He related to me that day the following story, which is taken from his most recent book *Hatch: Brainstorming Secrets of a Theme Park Designer.*

"When Michael Eisner asked us to brainstorm what he would like to build on the old Disneyland parking lot, I stepped to the big sheet where he had drawn two big circles. The top circle represented Disneyland Park, and the bottom circle, 100 acres of asphalt. I drew a quick pie-shaped wedge in the 11:00 o'clock position of the lower circle. 'Whatever we build, let's put a hotel inside of it.'

'Inside a theme park? Why?' asked a co-dreamer. But soon, they all got it. They were imagineers, after all."

Ironically, the idea of building a big resort hotel inside a theme park was unpopular at first, especially with the hotel builders and the management inside Disney, but it was, simply put, just too good not to work. The hotel would be built in exactly the same place visitors would come to play. It was location at its most logical.

From the opening of the park in 2001 to 2009, the hotel enjoyed one of the highest occupancy rates of any hotel in the Disney Empire. McNair told me that in 2009 Disney added 200 rooms and fifty vacation villas for Disney vacation club members. Now, that's a big idea.

We finished brunch, paid the bill, turned, and walked straight into California Adventure for a wonderful few hours of Disney fun. As a guest in the hotel, admission to the park is part of your room rate. As I was a guest of a guest, it was free for me.

"Come experience the magic of Disney for a few hours in between meetings" is a great slogan. And something I sure enjoyed doing!

I'm writing this while on an airplane traveling to a speaking engagement. I wish I were instead heading to California Adventure to become a kid again.

McNair Wilson, now an entrepreneur, had a big idea. Many big ideas, in fact. The Disney management realized they "should not keep him in captivity any longer. Time for him to be free."

> "The first element of an entrepreneurial leader that's really important to understand and identify is that every one of those individuals or groups of individuals has a big idea."

Are you a budding entrepreneur held captive inside corporate America? Are your big ideas also held captive? Just wondering. You should be too.

In this chapter, we will learn more of what makes one an entrepreneurial leader. What makes someone like my friend McNair Wilson, the perfect example of the main point of this chapter, tick?

The first element of an entrepreneurial leader that's really important to understand and identify is that every one of those individuals or groups of individuals has a big idea. You could root around in your briefcase and yank out an iPhone and you know right away that Steve Jobs of Apple had a brilliant idea. There aren't very many Steve Jobs' out there, but there are all kinds of smaller-scale versions of him, producing what seem to be little, bitty ideas that are actually really big ideas. You want to think, "What's mine?"

> "You've got to have a place where you actually create big ideas. If it doesn't start there, then nothing else happens later on."

The Womb Room

There's a place in my house that I call the Womb Room and it's a place where big ideas are conceived, gestate, and are nurtured into existence. Do you have such a place in your life? If you don't, you might want to think about creating one because if you're an entrepreneurial leader, you've got to have a place where you actually create big ideas. If it doesn't start there, then nothing else happens later on.

This is a picture of my Womb Room. When I need to get creative and find quiet time and space, as I did to write this book, I sit in that rocking chair, light the candle, open the shutters to let natural light in, and open my mind. This is a powerful place for me. You see,

that chair is a special chair. Growing up, I used to sit on that footstool and listen to my Grandfather Musick tell stories. Those times were treasures for a little boy. Now, as a 57-year-old man, I can still hear those stories. When Grandpa Musick ascended into heaven in 1976, he left me his favorite chair in his last will and testament. Notice how the chair covering doesn't match the rest of the décor of the office. It is the original fabric. When I sit in this chair, it's as if the spirit of my ancestor comes to sit with me.

This is a picture of my grandpa. He used to sit in that chair, roll his own cigarettes, gulp coffee from a mug the size of an urn, and pour his life into a seven-year-old boy. Me.

Grandpa lived close enough for me to ride my bike over just to hang out. Later, I would drive over. If I concentrate real hard, as I am right now, sitting in this chair, writing these words, I can almost smell the tobacco smoke. A powerful Womb Room indeed. I believe every person could create just such a place—a place where life is rich and big ideas are conceived.

Just for fun, send me photos of your creative spaces and tell me a little bit about them. I have a collection that I use for my class at DU. It's always fun to see where people come alive.

If you're a potential employee applying for a job in an entrepreneurial company, one of the things you want to do is to ask the entrepreneurial owner how he or she started the business. What was his or her big idea? Not many of us are going to get an opportunity to be able to have nose-to-nose conversations with Steve Jobs types, but what about somebody by the name of Bob Corn?

The 2012 election is now over and leadership decisions for the United States have been made. We watched the mainstream media print, blog, broadcast, and live stream the proclaimed coming disasters in bold print and neon lights. It's our company tradition to view the environment a little bit differently. And I started thinking that way long ago, after first interacting with a local business owner when I was just a boy.

In 1968 I met an entrepreneurial owner. His name was Bob Corn. I met him because he was kneeling on our kitchen floor, as if praying would bring our washing machine back to life. My mom and my dad were considering the washing machine to be dead on his arrival. They could spend $30 to buy a newly reconditioned machine from Mr. Corn. He told them that he could tear our existing washing machine apart and repair it for $12. Back in those days, Bob Corn would sell a brand-new, reconditioned machine for $35, and he would buy an old machine for $5. He would take the old machine away on the same day he delivered the new one.

Well, my family didn't have the $30. They opted for $12 with the promise from Bob that it would wash clothes for a good, long time. And if it broke, he'd come back and fix it, especially now that he intimately knew the machine, having torn it apart and put it back together.

I still remember the pat on the head and the hug he gave me as we walked out the back door, repairs completed, and a check in his hand. Most of all, though, I can still hear my mother's words: "There goes a man of utmost integrity. Remember what that feels like." All these years, I've remembered that encounter, though I was only twelve years old at the time.

Bob Corn had a big idea. He would take people's old washing machines and dryers that were so broken no one wanted them, and he would buy them for $5 apiece. Then he would turn them into treasures of rebuilt, reserviced washing machines. Now it doesn't get any more basic than that. You might never get an opportunity to talk with a major entrepreneur like Apple's Steve Jobs or Facebook's Mark Zuckerberg, but you could have a breakfast conversation with Bob Corn and talk to him about what's going on in his business now, 45 years later.

"That old business model, that old, brilliant idea, the big idea, is still as viable today as ever, and progressively adapting to new tools and technology."

And what is happening with his company now that I've grown up and he has gotten older too? Fast forward to his company in the present era, and you'll find that he has 11 people working for him. Some are full-time, others are part-time. There are three generations of Corns working in the family business and there's a little, bitty building that's about a block and a half from where he first started way back in 1968.

Now, as of this writing, he's hiring a brand-new, full-time equivalent for the old company. The reason that he's doing that is because his business has growing pains. He really needs to be able to find the right kind of people to come in and work in his company because his company is growing. To be sure, the company's on the World Wide Web. They surf Craigslist looking for old appliances to buy and rebuild for resale just as they always did. That old business model, that old, brilliant idea, the big idea, is still as viable today as ever, and progressively adapting to new tools and technology, rather than operating simply by word of mouth, as it was back in 1968 when my parents first hired him.

They also have a coveted sales contract with Whirlpool to provide commercial coin-operated and large industrial laundry equipment to apartment buildings, hotels, hospitals, and heavy industrial users. They obtained the contract because of their long history of integrity in the community as a small business. Now that's a big idea.

Bob Corn told me, "When you wear the uniform of Arvada Appliance on the back, hold your head up because we're part of an upright company." That's more than their motto. It's an operational imperative. It wins business over the long haul. His company doesn't show up in neon lights. It doesn't show up in big, bold print above the fold in newspaper articles. They just go about doing their regular business. They are successful and growing, and my response to that story is that many other little, bitty businesses are like that in America. How many Bob Corns are there? The answer is millions. It's one of the things that make our business community so productive. It's what makes America America.

The only thing in bold print, in neon lights, is an "Open" sign in his store window. It's flicked on at 8:00 a.m. Imagine that? A retail appliance store open at 8:00 a.m. There isn't a lot of flash to that business. But there is a lot of hard work. Arvada Appliance is just one of those businesses in America that employs a dozen people and takes care of families. They don't need polished floors. They don't need fancy stuff. They just need the materials to do a good job for their clients, whether corporations or a family trying to stretch budget dollars.

We have talked about Apple and we have talked about Disney, both major international companies that anyone in the world will recognize. Still, it is the small companies like Arvada Appliance, providing everyday services that are the backbone of this book, and the backbone of job growth in America. Everybody relates to an appliance store run by a family and what that can mean for a community, for people who rely on having their appliances repaired and working as soon as possible after they break down.

When you think about being an entrepreneur, what's your big idea? This guy, Bob Corn, turned trash into treasure. His cost of goods, his raw material, is $5, at least in 1968 terms. He puts in some labor and effort and he sells the product for $35. That kind of margin is a thriving business, I don't care where you are. We're talking really basic stuff: washing machines. You could also apply that business model to all kinds of other enterprises and business, but that was Bob Corn's big idea.

> "When you think about being an entrepreneur, what's your big idea?"

The big question is, "What's yours? What's your big idea?"

It's worth some womb-room time to figure that out.

In Bob's case, he has a particular gift. He loves people, and he's one of those guys who can fix anything that's broken, and he blended both of those qualities together in a business enterprise that, after 45 years, is now in a transition to the next generation that's going to take that business and make it go to the stratosphere because of the Internet and the accelerating power of technology.

The first element of understanding entrepreneurial leaders is to know their big idea. How did they get their start and how does that express itself in the business they are running?

If you have a great idea that is truly a big idea, or on its way to becoming one, flesh it out. Take the time to figure out what your big idea is and why. If you're an employee and you're interviewing with a business organization, you really want to know what the business's big idea is so you can figure out if that's something that you want to participate in. Is it an idea, a company, that you would want to work for? Understanding that first big idea, that creative genius, is the essence. It's the beginning of a journey .

EL

Do you have a Womb Room? Is there a location available where you can simply listen quietly to the yearnings of your own soul? Is your big idea in need of a polish in the same way that a soft cloth removes the tarnish from the silver tea set that's been handed down from generation to generation—that soft cloth restoring the luster and the value of something cherished? Is it time to go back to your first love and conjure up maybe a new, brilliant idea to energize your business?

UW

Unsecured workers, out on a search like a naval war ship hunting submarines, earnestly seeking to secure the right job, should look at small and medium-sized entrepreneurial organizations and ask them about their big idea. Specifically, how did the founder/owner discover the driving force, the big idea of the organization? Few prospective employees ask that question, and all founders/owners are warmed right down to their toes when asked to recount the genesis of their big idea. Asking that question will separate an applicant from all the others in the crowded field of applicants, and creating separation in an interview situation is where the marrow is.

CHAPTER 3

Entrepreneurial Element Two: Who Benefits and by How Much?

PAIN ———————————————————————— **PLEASURE**

MARKETING MOVEMENT

When you think about a big idea, the very next thought you should have is who will benefit from your big idea. And it isn't just a matter of who benefits. It's a matter of determining why they will benefit from your idea. It can be an excitement and a desire and a benefit above and beyond where they are now, or it can be an advantage, something to alleviate pain.

The difference between pain alleviation and excitement and desire will determine the economic altitude of your idea.

There are products that alleviate pain or create a desire, a massive driving force. An example of that in today's market would be a social-media-driven product that goes viral and remains commercially viable long enough to monetize the residual value for optimal benefit. This is sometimes referred to as the long tail business strategy.

We've all seen a flash in the pan, a fad that didn't have any legs. Well, your big idea will be realized in such a way that it actually does have legs.

Here is an idea that went viral a long time ago, way back in 1964.

In that year, a young couple named Anne and Mike Moore came back home to America from their Peace Corps field work in Africa. They were forced to come home from the country of Togo because Anne was eight months pregnant. Any further along in her pregnancy than that and she would not have been allowed to fly. Four weeks after returning home, Anne Moore walked out of Denver's Porter Hospital with her first daughter, Mandela, strapped to her back in the same way babies are carried in Africa.

That might seem a common image in America now, but at the time, it was nothing short of revolutionary, if not downright shocking.

The Moores were tasked to work in health-care communities in Africa. One of the things they noticed was the high level of children's safety and security, which was remarkable compared to US practices in 1964.

The reason is the way that African women carry their children. They literally wrap them tight and strap them to their backs, as if they were in a back pack. Anne and Mike adopted that idea with their own baby, and when they walked out of the hospital, the health-care people stopped them and asked, "What are you doing?" It was so unusual. And thus the Snugli was born.

The original Snugli now resides in the Smithsonian Museum. It was based on the idea of the mother holding her child close. Flexibility was built into the product so that a mother could be active with other tasks while, at the same time, taking care of her baby.

The Moores sold their Snuglis individually, mostly through health-care workers at Porter Hospital. And they were made one by one. The Moores came from the Dunkers, German Baptists who live like the better-known Amish of Pennsylvania and Ohio, simple, wholesome people—hands to work, minds to God.

The Moores' business was at first a cottage industry. By 1966 they had 150 women in Ohio, making Snuglis by hand, one by one by one. In 1969, Baby News stores ordered 100 units. In 1975 Consumer Reports published an article. The *Wall Street Journal* picked it up. And the Moores moved their production to a manufacturing facility to keep up with the pace.

They built the manufacturing facility in Colorado. In 1975, what we get is the old classic image of the hockey stick on the growth chart. Their company just started to mushroom.

In 1980 they developed a Korean supply chain, manufacturing Snuglis in Korea and shipping them to the United States. In 1985 they sold Snugli to Huffy, which was an infant textile company.

Snugli was an organization that the Moores started from an idea they had in Africa. And they intuitively understood that their market was young women who wanted to hold their babies close, heartbeat against heartbeat, and still be unencumbered so that they could do all kinds of other things at the same time.

There are now dozens of different Snugli styles. If you go into a Motherhood Maternity shop or similar stores, you see them there everywhere. The Moores were people who had a big idea but also understood who their market was and who benefited.

> "In 1975, what we get is the old classic image of the hockey stick on the growth chart. Their company just started to mushroom."

> "The Moores were people who had a big idea but also understood who their market was and who benefitted."

It's a simple question that all entrepreneurs should ask themselves: how does their market benefit from what they've created?

It's the secret to creating wealth, and boy, the Moores sure did that. That story talks about understanding your market and creating a niche for yourself as an entrepreneur. The Snugli story does both.

It's a pain alleviator and it's also a reward for moms—and dads too—that keeps kids close to them.

Every woman in my generation is going to say, "Oh, yeah, I had one of those!" I mean, it was absolutely the rage.

The story of Mike and Anne Moore of Evergreen, Colorado, also shows that an idea can come from anywhere. It can come from around the corner. It can come from a trip around the world—Africa, in this case.

After you get a great big idea and you have something creative, the very next step on the entrepreneurial ladder is figuring out who benefits from your big idea. You must figure out who your customers will be. The strength of their desire for your big idea will determine the financial altitude of your company.

You must ask, "How can my big idea create a wow factor for customers? Does it give them an endorphins-and-enkephalins-in-their-brain kind of high? Does it give them a thrill and excitement, or is it an antidote to pain?" Relating your big idea to some kind of emotional hook will drive your ideas.

Benefits of Your Big Idea

Being able to take your big idea and understand who benefits and how strong that benefit is comprises the second element in the entrepreneurial process. For example, if we go to the smartphone that you dragged out of your purse, your briefcase, or your pocket, it isn't hard to figure out who benefits from that. It's one of the reasons that Apple has long been considered one of the most important companies in the world in terms of product innovation.

A Snugli is another product with clear benefits for specific users. A Snugli is basically a backpack, a harness that you would wear in front of you or on your back so that that you can carry your baby around with you, comfortably, wherever you go.

I would ask you, "What about this product? Who benefits from that big idea?" Another question I would ask is "Who loves that item and why?" The people who love Snuglis are active women who love their kids and want to keep their kids close to them and still be active and productive. That's the Snugli market. The Snugli is an example of who benefits from the big idea, how strong the motivation is, and how big the problem is that the Snugli solves.

> "Entrepreneurial leaders are exceptionally good at mental gymnastics."

Customer Focus

The Snugli was a smashing success because it was very specific in terms of customer orientation. That's the second element in any entrepreneurial creative process. If you don't have a customer focus, if you don't know who benefits from your big idea, it's not a big idea. You've got to figure out who benefits. That's part of the creative process but it's also a developmental one.

This section explains that entrepreneurial leaders must ask themselves who benefits from their big idea and why. Then they must ask the next question: "How do you get to them?" We're talking about customer orientation: where is your market, and how you are going to get your big idea in front of that market. That requires mental gymnastics. Entrepreneurial leaders are exceptionally good at mental gymnastics.

If you're an unsecured worker, ask your entrepreneurial interviewer to describe in detail whom his business serves and what the enterprise's marketing strategy is. If an entrepreneurial organization can't answer those two questions, would you want to work there? Remember, we're talking about securing the right job, not just any job.

EL The take-away value for an **entrepreneurial leader** is in the rigors of managing the day to day. Did your business drift off course? How long has it been since you thoroughly reviewed how your big idea applies to your current customer base? Has your customer base also drifted? Are these and other potential changes factored in to your planning? Do you need to think about changing your marketing tactics because the market place is changing? The illustration at the beginning of this chapter is important. Identifying where the typical customer is on that line and thinking about how your business generates *movement* will determine the altitude of the economics of any business. The greater the distance your business can move a customer along that line, the greater will be your financial reward.

UW **Unsecured workers** should ask why current customers buy the organization's product or service. What drives them? Is it to solve a problem or is it to actualize a visceral desire? Again, asking this kind of question in an interview can separate you from the others in the crowded field of employment seekers. Such questions will let the entrepreneur know that you are the right person to hire.

CHAPTER 4

Entrepreneurial Element Three: Fantastic People

The third element of entrepreneurial leadership is that entrepreneurs surround themselves with fantastic people. It might surprise many that, in my 37 years of working with entrepreneurial businesses and in my own practice, I have found this element to be the hardest part of entrepreneurial success. Managing the people side of a business is one of the biggest issues facing entrepreneurs. Discovering, selecting, training, developing, evaluating the performance of personnel, and retaining long-term this vital resource is a huge challenge for entrepreneurial owners and their employees.

> "Managing the people side of a business is one of the biggest issues facing entrepreneurs."

As a general rule, entrepreneurial leaders are not very patient. It's one of the reasons they are successful. They don't have the inclination to build teams. They just know what they want and they want it yesterday. On the other hand, human resource management needs the quintessential team building/project management mentality. A good company needs both sets of skills. A successful entrepreneur needs a "polar opposite" to balance out his/her skills. So who works with me? Who's my polar opposite?

Patricia Kramer walked into our business in 1983, the sixth year of our operation. She was 35 years old at the time, with teenage sons, and she was looking for full-time employment just as she was getting ready to send her sons to college. She was herself the daughter of an entrepreneur.

Patricia was born and raised in a small, rural, eastern Colorado, farm community. She had a two-year associate's degree in business administration. Under her photo in her high-school yearbook, was her personal motto, "If I can't find a way, I'll make one." I think she worked for me for about two years, and then we transitioned to her working *with* me because she had gifts and talents far beyond my capabilities.

Destiny Capital would not be where it is today without this woman. She's the ultimate, consummate people manager and operations project manager. She's really, really good at what she does. I'm really, really good at what I do too, and together we built a business.

In 1995, a brokerage technology operation came to us and asked us if we wanted to be part of a study group that would beta test new technology in exchange for a platform to trade on the New York Stock Exchange to be used by independent advisors. Prior to that time the stock exchanges were dominated by large institutions. There just wasn't any direct access for small, entrepreneurial, independent firms like Destiny Capital. It was a trading platform, essentially, built to allow technology to level the playing field of Wall Street. I said, "Not on your life." I didn't want to be a part of that. All I saw was trouble. When I listened to their presentation to us, all I saw were these techies with a boondoggle and for us, as a small company, lots of resources being poured down the drain. Even as entrepreneurial as I was, I couldn't see the benefit. They didn't move me along the pain-to-pleasure line discussed in the previous chapter.

Pat Kramer looked at their offer and said, "Oh, yes, we would like to do it. Absolutely, we want to do that." We're now in the eleventh iteration of that trading system. It's the trading system that's currently used by the Bank of New York Mellon for its entire independent operation.

We get the use of it for a flat fee every year. It's now a central and strategic advantage for Destiny Capital's business and its clients. We own it outright in perpetuity as long as we meet our regulatory requirements and our solvency standards. We wouldn't have any of that were it not for Pat Kramer.

Do you have a Pat Kramer working inside your organization? She took the opportunity to train other people to use the system, and then supervised its implementation. It's now integrated into everything that we do. She's a detailed people person, whereas I'm a big-picture, strategic person. We complement one another.

Do you have somebody in your organization who is like that—an alter ego? As an entrepreneur, I need a strong personality. It comes with the package. I need somebody to help me run the company and be a buffer. I'm not exactly easy to work with.

When I talked to Pat Kramer about mentioning this in the book, she said, "Well, frankly, you're a little bit exasperating." I love her honesty.

But she added, "We worked through it," because, she said, "you do things that I can't do, and I do things that you need."

The scripture verse reads, "Don't let the sun go down on your anger." We really implemented that in our business, so that if we upset one another—and we have, and we do, and we will—we never let the door close on a day of business and be angry.

We resolve it. We settle it. And Pat Kramer fosters resolution, which is both the antidote and support for the strong personality of an entrepreneurial business leader.

Who's going to be your company's Pat Kramer?

> "A people manager is a counterbalance to the typically strong personality of an entrepreneurial leader."

I'm going to put on my entrepreneurial leader hat for a minute. I want to suggest that both you, as an entrepreneurial leader, and your business, would benefit from a people manager, a person who is a counterbalance to the typically strong personality of an entrepreneurial leader. Strength through diversity.

For thirty years at our little company, Destiny Capital, an alter ego has been at my right hand, someone who is the consummate people person. It's one of the reasons that our company is successful and has achieved what it's achieved. Pat Kramer and I balance each other out exceptionally well. Left to my own devices, I would have destroyed this company years ago.

Entrepreneurial leaders often find it extremely difficult to share responsibility with another person. I think it's essential for a company to have legs so it has longevity. If you're an unsecured worker looking for a job, a diversified team-management style should be a key ingredient to look for in an entrepreneurial organization. You should try to invest time in interviews with both the entrepreneurial leader and the people manager, however those roles are designated, because those executives are really alter egos, telling you from their own perspectives how the company is run.

Strategic Work Teams

Well-managed companies are often organized into strategic work teams. Having the teams conduct interviews of new applicants as well as giving the applicants an up-close and personal view of the organization is, I believe, extraordinarily effective. If I were interested in working in an organization and I were in an interview, I would want to be introduced to the people with whom I'd be working closely and I'd want to have an interview with them. That would give me a good idea of whether the business is well managed. Is it the real deal or not? You need to ask questions of potential coworkers to see if a business environment is right for you, as well as to know if the company, and therefore your potential job, has long-term viability along with room for growth.

One of the issues that entrepreneurial leaders deal with is the constant turnover of staff. Type-A driver-drivers may drive their people nuts. Hard to accept, but very often true. If entrepreneurial leaders continuously burn through employees, they may need an alter ego to help manage their company.

> "People are the sustainable source of competitive advantage in the marketplace."

Another aspect of hiring great people is compensation. Workers are worthy of their wages. Productive workers are also worthy to share in the results of their productivity. Many business consultants and advisors view compensation as purely a financial decision. It is much more than that. It is a resource allocation to maintain and improve the vital resource of the business. People are the sustainable source of competitive advantage in the marketplace.

The standard compensation matrix starts out with some kind of base salary—and maybe a sales commission and bonuses if you're in sales—and then the next level up would be paid time off versus sick leave and vacation. The idea is that you receive a certain number of vacation days and, on top of that, you receive a certain number of sick days.

I take that a step further; I say, as manager of my own business, "It's all paid time off." If you don't get sick, you add your unclaimed sick days to your vacation days, and the combined personal days, vacation days, and sick days are all counted as paid time off. That virtually eliminates that the problem of employees who take a sick day, although they're actually not sick, because they want to go to the ball game. It gives people an incentive to perform well. If they want to take a day off and go to the ball game, they can; it's legitimate paid time off. This is a great way to effectively manage people and allow them to understand their worth to the company is appreciated.

Benefits Buffet

We structure benefits—and I believe all companies should do this—as though they were a buffet line where employees could take some of this and some of that. My employees can choose their benefits a la carte because different employees need different benefits. Modern technology allows really small companies to do that. I call it the "benefits buffet." You can do the same kind of thing with retirement plans.

One of the keys to managing great people is gain sharing. The whole concept of gain sharing is about everybody in the organization sharing, in an equitable manner, the productivity of the group.

This is the Nash theory written very small for entrepreneurial companies. Think of the movie *A Beautiful Mind*, starring Russell Crowe, about the mathematician John Nash. Ron Howard, the director of the movie, did an absolutely powerful job describing the Nash theory and its relevance to choices that benefit a group of people working together. I apply it here to a small business with the idea that you've got to be able to run your accounting system such that you can calculate progress and productivity; you have to create a system in which you can equitably share the results of your productivity with the whole staff, from the newest hire to the person who has been there the longest.

This topic of human resource management is the most difficult for entrepreneurs to embrace. The entrepreneurial leader feels he or she is giving up control and transferring emotional and financial equity and cash flow. But managed well, this element is actually the largest catalytic accelerator of the business.

When was the last time you disconnected from your enterprise? How long were you gone? What was it like when you came back? How long did it take for your business to return to normal? Were you ready emotionally to come back? What has been the turnover rate of your workforce over the last one, three, and five years?

> **People doing most what they do best generates optimal economic results."**

People doing most what they do best generates optimal economic results. People are the sustainable source of competitive advantage in the market place.

Let me move on to the unsecured worker. This area is as challenging for the unsecured worker as it is for the entrepreneurial leader. Loyalty from organizations to their workforces has diminished over the years. It seems every month the airwaves are populated with another sordid tale of organizational chicanery. It's part of why I believe small and medium-sized companies will be the next megatrend in American business.

Can you, as an unsecured worker, exhibit the characteristics of a stakeholder? Can you bring a mindset that encapsulates the Nash theory? Just for grins go watch the movie *A Beautiful Mind*. Really focus on the scene in the bar with the men looking for love from the gorgeous blonde. It's an especially good illustration of the Nash theory. John Nash was given the Nobel Prize for this theory, which holds that in a negotiated setting the parties that seek the best outcome for themselves and for the group at large are the parties that win. Finding, maybe creating, such a place in your organization changes the nature of the work. It enhances the quality of life of the organization and of the people who work there, and it enhances their personal quality of life as well.

Reconsider the practice of interviewing for jobs and instead start conversations to become stakeholders of thriving fantastic organizations that you want to work with. If you change your mind, you'll probably change your life. I believe people are going about their job searches in the wrong way. This is part of the issue in the financial crisis and the downturn. We are all going to wear this emotional scar for a long time. And the people, the unsecured workers, who actually make the quantum shift in their thinking will carry the day for themselves and for the country as a whole. We are talking about the culture of trust which has taken quite a beating over the last decade.

Another element—that I will explain with an illustration grid— is one we have here at Destiny Capital. It is a function of years of service and base salary. Different people show up in different places on the grid. (Please see page 49 for a sample of how a grid can operate.) Every 90 days we take a certain amount of our profits and we set it aside in a profit-sharing pool. It is distributed quarterly to everybody who works in our enterprise so they have a specific line of sight between what they do every day and the results that are generated every quarter. The biggest determinant in the calculation is client satisfaction.

The last piece of our compensation matrix is continuing education, training, and reimbursement, which means we invest in our resource and we encourage our staff to get better, whether that's through education or training or some kind of professional development that helps them do their job better. Continuing education and training gives my employees the ability to raise their base salary. As their base salary goes up, everything else in the matrix also rises. Their gain share gets bigger. Their benefits are larger. Their retirement plan contributions are bigger. They get more paid time off—all of that.

> "Empower people to virtually create their own job description and their own value to the organization. When they improve, the company improves."

When you do this, you empower people to virtually create their own job description and their own value to the organization. When they improve, the company improves too.

The philosophy is that the base salary is determined by the marketplace. I'm going to pay employees in New York differently from employees in Omaha, Nebraska. The knowledge, the skills, and abilities required for a specific job are also going to be a factor.

For example, at Destiny Capital, we set all of our base salaries just a little bit below—not much, but a little bit below—the local market, maybe 5 percent. Any member of our organization can transition to another company for a salary raise. My job as the entrepreneurial leader is to develop a human resource and a culture that give my employees maximal career altitude and freedom. It's my challenge, then, to create a working environment, a culture, no one would want to leave. It's the idea that we develop employees to the point where they could go anywhere they wanted to go and make more money, but instead, they have absolutely no desire to leave.

Equitable Gain Sharing

Equitable gain sharing is a critical part of that productivity. It's the glue that holds our company together. In your bathroom, it'd be the grout between the tiles. Now after 37 years, we've had minimal turnover. It's one of the reasons why we have a compounding company. It's because we have compounded people. We continue to grow and get better. That's true of huge numbers of large organizations. It's not as true in small entrepreneurial companies, but I say that it could be. In my view, it would be an absolute key to an entrepreneurial business that wants to grow to the next level and it has to do with how that business manages its human resource.

Gain Sharing Illustration Assuming $100,000 Net Income

Net Income (Before Distribution)			$ 100,000		
Gross distributable income			$ 25,000		
Company's share of payroll taxes			$ (1,713) (About 7.65% of $22,391)		
Company's 401k match			$ (896) (Assume 4% match)		
Net distribution to employees			$ 22,391		

Employee	Base Comp	Years of Service	Points	Gain Share Per Cent	Employee Share
A	32	2	34	4.7%	$ 1,044.30
B	27	4	31	4.3%	$ 952.16
C	77	6	83	11.4%	$ 2,549.32
D	60	8	68	9.3%	$ 2,088.60
E	43	10	53	7.3%	$ 1,627.88
F	38	12	50	6.9%	$ 1,535.73
G	70	14	84	11.5%	$ 2,580.03
H	40	16	56	7.7%	$ 1,720.02
I	55	18	73	10.0%	$ 2,242.17
J	90	20	110	15.1%	$ 3,378.61
K	65	22	87	11.9%	$ 2,672.18
			729	100%	$ 22,391.00

1. Assign points to each employee as follows:
   1 point for each $1,000 of salary (Base Comp);
   1 point for each year of service.
2. Accumulate total points for each employee.
3. Calculate total points.
4. Calculate % of total points designated for each employee. The result is the per cent of total profit sharing to be allocated to each employee.
5. Each quarter, calculate net income before distribution to employees. This should be the same as your net income on the income statement (profit and loss statement).
6. Gross distributable income will be 25% of that total. Gross distributable profit is the cost of the distribution to the company.
7. Calculate the company cost of the distribution. That will normally consist of the company's share of payroll taxes. If the company pays matching 401(k), that should also be included in the cost.
8. Subtract the company cost of the distribution from the gross distributable profit. That gives you the amount of net distribution which will be paid to the employees according to their gain sharing per cent.

GAIN SHARING MATRIX

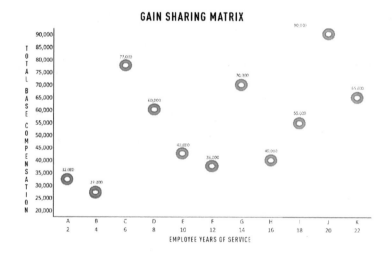

Toxic versus Healthy Work Environments

As an unsecured worker, if you ask open-ended questions in an interview with multiple interviewers, you will have the ability to taste a toxic environment; you'll be able to ask yourself, "Do I really like these people?" If you're in a multiple-interview situation and you're talking to many people, very few will be able to lie to you more than once, unless you're interviewing in a company that's a cult, as for example, the one in John Grisham's novel *The Firm*.

I also want to emphasize to those of you who are seeking jobs the importance of making yourself stand out, especially when so many people are going for the same job, as is the case in today's economy. I hear from many young people about the number of interviews they go through at one company. The research backs up this phenomenon. For every available job, there are now five qualified candidates. Part of what you're experiencing is that nobody among those five has created enough separation between himself or herself and the competition for the company management to be able to say, "Oh my God. This person is the real deal. I ought to hire her tomorrow." In a way, you unsecured workers in the interviewing process are still auditioning; there's still an opening in the cast, and you've got to convince the people at the audition that you can actually perform. Then you've got to convince yourself as well. How do you do that? By understanding your strengths and weaknesses. It's good for you to know what you're extremely good at along with the areas where you might need help.

Part of what you're looking for when interviewing with a company is their evaluating process. How do they develop you? How do they evaluate your performance? What's their feedback loop to you? That's management 101. Yet many companies don't think about this, nor do those who interview for the open positions.

I will tell you that this last six- or seven-year economic downturn has created horrific work environments. There's a general sense of impermanence in the marketplace: "As soon as this thing turns around, I'm out of here." Part of this book's purpose is to help people realize their potential: "I now have tools I need to secure the right job, because I've been working in the wrong place for the last five years and it's killing me." I know that to be true because I've heard it from the people I serve in my company and from being in the marketplace.

EL

If you're an **entrepreneurial leader,** who is your alter-ego people manager? If you're that leader, the one you see in the mirror each morning when you're putting on your make-up or shaving, consider finding one. More than likely, the altitude of your enterprise will be tied to that alter ego. Having such a member of staff will also make your life more relaxed and less hectic as you work to grow your company.

If you have another alter ego, is that position at the C-level of your organizational chart? Is that person a chief people officer, in the way you have a chief financial officer and a chief executive officer? How much authority and responsibility do you give that person? Unless I'm mistaken, the next big surge coming in America is going to be organizations that manage their human resources very differently from how we have up to now. How much turnover is your company currently enduring? As an entrepreneurial leader, are you measuring that, and should you?

UW

If you're an **unsecured worker,** evaluate prospective organizations on more than just pure job description and salary ranges. Consider looking more deeply into the full company culture and look for gain-sharing opportunities. It will help if the company has a system of strategic work teams. Then, you can interview with the people you'll work with closely to find out if they are a good fit for you.

Use multiple data points in your interviews with the company. If the company uses strategic work teams, everybody you talk to on the team is a data point. If you're interviewing in an entrepreneurial business and you're only interviewing with one person, I think that's a mistake. You want multiple data points. Talk to the human resources director and then talk to other people in the organization and interview them.

Continued on next page...

Some people are uncomfortable with that, but that actually will be one of the key factors separating you from everybody else who's hunting for a job. The difference is that you're trying to secure the right job, not just any job. The fact that you walk into an interview with that mindset is incredibly distinctive. Isn't standing out what you're looking for? If you're in an interview, you're really trying to figure out, "How do I stand out?" This is a big one in my opinion and in my experience. I train my university students in this. It's effective interviewing and it's an important aspect of entrepreneurial company building.

Office politics are the polar opposite of organizational productivity. When the compensation system is fully integrated with the strategic business plan, the subterranean office dynamics are muted. They seldom disappear altogether, but when eight members of a team are all working together making progress, the one person not operating in concert with the others really stands out. When gain sharing is based on the entire team's productivity, the incentive to perform is a unifying factor. The team itself becomes self-modifying. When one team member is not carrying the proper load and the gain sharing of the entire unit is at stake, the operative norm is for the others to work with the one who is falling behind and encourage that person to carry his or her own weight. If that corrective action doesn't work, the next corrective step is to give the manager of the unit the authority to fix the problem. The culture of our organization removes the subterranean behavior, not allowing it to take root and grow into a problem within Destiny Capital.

During multiple interviews, you should ask short questions and spend a lot of time listening to the conversation. The conversation that you, as an interviewee, get from the multiple data points is going to give you some real clues about what it would be like to actually work in that business. I think you should feed open-ended questions to people and just listen to the answers and take notes. I would be a very active listener in that environment.

CHAPTER 5

Entrepreneurial Element Four: Laser Beam Focus

The fourth element of an entrepreneurial mind comes from element number one, the big idea. This is a specific, laser beam focus on what customers are saying. We touched on that a little bit in a previous chapter. This element requires painstaking drilling down, down, and down. No, not enough yet. Further, further, deeper still.

What are the specific drivers to your specific business?

> **It's** not enough to have a big idea."

It's not enough to have a big idea. It's not enough to know who your customers are. You've got to really understand what is driving those customers to your business. Being very specific about the strength of the drivers will determine the financial and economic altitude of your company. Tom Peters and Bob Waterman in their 1982 book *In Search of Excellence* dedicated an entire chapter to this idea. They call it "stick to your knitting"—in other words, doing what you do best, and it's been proven right for a long time. It has to do with the entrepreneur actually thinking about what he or she is doing and figuring out how to do it better. Some people will say you really want to diversify your product offerings. You want to diversify your business. You want to cross-sell your activities. My response to that is: as long as it doesn't detract from your big idea and the laser beam focus, it is okay. Frankly, if you do diversify, you're really talking about a separate idea. You're talking about a totally new big idea and you have to go through a separate process for that separate big idea. It doesn't mean that you can't have two. It just means that if you diversify at the expense of your central big idea, you're probably making a mistake.

> "We should exploit comparative advantage, which is to do most that which you absolutely do the best."

Remember the story that I told earlier about Arvada Appliance. I find it fascinating that this company is now surfing Craigslist to find old washing machines to buy for a song and rehab and then turn around and sell. The company is still operating, after 44 years, using the same business model it started with. I think there's genius in that. Now, they've also done all kinds of other things that have really helped the company to grow, but it's been **in addition to**, not in lieu of, what's already worked well for them. They are using new technology to help them, searching the web in addition to word of mouth, but the technology continues the same process they have always had.

A recent book by Jim Collins, the 2001 *Good to Great*, contains an entire section on this idea. He calls it the "hedgehog"—simplifying a complex world into a single organizing idea. It's like "stick to your knitting." It's the specific focus of a business unit or a business big idea. The economist in me says that we should exploit comparative advantage, which is to do most that which you absolutely do the best. You want to exploit that to the fullest extent possible what you do best with your business, with your big idea.

Entrepreneurial leaders have a laser-beam focus. Entrepreneurial leaders are by nature creative in their design, and they're notorious for creating all kinds of multiple big ideas. I think a lot of entrepreneurs are closet ADD—Attention Deficit Disorder—people. Their brilliance can also be a great detriment to an organization because they end up doing multiple things not as effectively and not as well as they could, which ultimately affects their finances and their economics.

We all know that enterprises have designed, built, and staffed entire divisions only later to discover that they were actually diversions from the laser focus of known productivity. These things become rabbit trails and sidebars leading to the utter destruction of companies.

While I was in the process of doing research and gathering data for this book, the headlines in the financial community were in full-reporting mode on an eye-popping merger. A mining conglomerate, Freeport McMoRan Copper & Gold, would acquire Plains Exploration and McMoRan Exploration, both oil exploration companies.

All commodities, right? The Freeport leadership could not offer synergies from combining a mining company and two oil drilling organizations to justify the economics of the transaction. As I listened in on the investor conference conversations (these are open web casts to the general public and are part of our normal research work), the managerial economist inside me screamed, "Rabbit trail!"

My personal opinion is the acquiring company lost the laser beam focus driving the enterprise. The rating agencies also weighed in on the merger, downgrading the combined company debt to negative from neutral on concerns about the extra debt needed to finance the transaction. The trading machine on Wall Street didn't wait long either, creating selling pressure sufficient to drive the company value on the New York Stock Exchange from 38.28 on December 4, 2012, to 30.81 on December 6, 2013. The value chart in the following months looked like an EKG of a very unhealthy cardiac patient. Total value destruction was in the billions—a high cost of losing managerial focus.

There are many examples of companies going astray, turning away from their true core identity and bankrupting themselves in the process. When a company specializes in one thing, itself very complex, and tries to add another exceedingly complex company into the mix, it's a recipe for disaster. It can potentially impact stock value, along with the everyday running of a company that might have already been successful. In some ways, it is unbelievable to see this on such a grand scale. If the Freeport managers had read my book, they would have saved all that money for their existing shareholders, not to mention their employees.

On a positive note, there are companies like Airlift, which deals with mobile oxygen units. It's an example of an organization that diversified its product offering, but only after it fully developed the first one. And who was behind it? A couple we already know well from Snugli. Interestingly enough, it used a very similar principle: placing all the oxygen needs into a small pouch that can be worn as a backpack, just like their most famous, earlier product. Then they used the same growth and marketing techniques they learned at Snugli. Airlift has now been sold to a major corporation.

I am also intimately familiar with another company here in Denver that chose not to diversify and is all the better for it. A number of years ago, a client of mine had an opportunity to modernize his business operation and his factory. By modernize, I mean that, for the first time, he was going to bring computer automated robotics to the manufacturing process. The change reflected two things: It was exceptionally productive and it was also exceptionally risky because for some 20-odd years, he had run an organization that did custom woodworking. They were turning a custom process over to a computerized, robotic-driven one, not quite an assembly line but pretty close. The cost of automation was significant.

The person at that company who programs and operates the computerized router designed the program to create the item in this picture on the left. He did it in his spare time, just for fun. That wooden toy, made from scrap wood, fits together tightly without any glue. This tells you a great deal about the capability of the robotics system, huh?

One of the selling points of this big machine my client was considering buying was that it would allow him, with a simple change of drill bits and materials, to use not just wood but also plastics, along with metals, and to some extent, ceramics, in theory giving him the potential to expand his business.

Yet he decided, twelve years ago, not to expand his business because, after all of the years he'd been in business, he knew what he was good at. For example, people would send him pictures of products they wanted him to make. With all of his experience and talent, he would be able look at the photograph or drawing or thumbnail sketch in hand, run it through his head, and say, "I think it'd cost this much in wood, this much in materials, this much in labor, and I think it's going to cost about that to do this." All of this instant knowledge was based on his years of specialization in one thing only: wood.

> "Exploiting your comparative advantage, is a great way to survive when a lot of other companies don't."

We developed computer systems that would help him do cost analysis. It's pretty amazing that his estimates were almost as good as anything the computer could calculate. It became a very good checks-and-balances system for him and his bidding process that made sure the work he did on the shop floor would actually show up in his bank account.

My client decided to stay in wood because, as he put it, "I know wood. I know different kinds of wood. I've spent my life around wood. I do not want to get involved in plastics or metals or any other material because I don't know that." That's an example of a laser beam focus.

That company is one of only two custom woodworking manufacturers in Denver that are still alive. One of the reasons my client's business is still alive is the computer automation and robotics program we installed at his company twelve years ago. We're going to expand his factory and put in a second machine because he's so busy. In the middle of the great recession he is growing! Having a laser beam focus for your business and sticking to your knitting, exploiting your comparative advantage, is a great way to survive when a lot of other companies don't. If you're an entrepreneurial leader, you want to be able to go back through and quickly understand your laser beam focus because it will quickly reveal if you've got diversions in your business that are unhealthy. You'll know right away, and your organization will then focus on doing the right things extraordinarily well.

For unsecured workers: When researching entrepreneurial leadership companies, can you easily determine the company's business model? Can you see the laser beam? Can you see the specifics of what it is that the company does and what it does really well and is it repeatable? If not, ask about it at your interview. You want to be able to understand what this company is actually really good at and why.

Again, as an unsecured worker, what you're trying to do is create separation between you and everybody else who's applying for the job. Understanding this element makes you distinctive among the unemployed masses. That applies to all kinds of different businesses. It's a universal construct.

Having a laser beam focus—that's the fourth element of an entrepreneurial mind.

The other thing I would add in the case of my client is that he's still in business because what he does cannot be outsourced to China—shipping the wood out there, having Chinese workers make the product, shipping it back, and competing with him on price. You just can't do it. He doesn't lose any business at all to outsourcing and international competition. None.

I would say also that one of the megatrends happening right now and, I think, one that will continue to grow, is the insourcing of entrepreneurial manufacturing in the United States for competitive cost and high quality. That's part of the entrepreneurial surge that I see coming. I don't think that's going to happen with massive organizations. I think you're going to see that with small- and medium-sized groups and it won't be just technology and microchips. It'll be all kinds of products and services. There are particular parts of the country where this is even being created as a brand, for instance, the Made in Brooklyn trend, or the return of manufacturing to the South, happening in Mississippi and Alabama today. The biggest problem with some companies in Birmingham, Alabama, is their lack of sufficient staff because manufacturing organizations are moving into town in droves and they're siphoning off some of their high-quality talent. When was the last time that was true?

In California there is also a rather massive example: American Apparel. It makes very simple clothing, easily manufactured, and it's part of the urban chic sensibility. This trend of a return to manufacturing in the United States is happening coast to coast. It's not an isolated, Denver-only example. Entrepreneurs are the ones seizing on this trend, and you need to understand them.

EL This discussion in this chapter is about the laser beam focus of the entrepreneurial mindset, the entrepreneurial leader takeaway. Since you are already an **entrepreneurial leader**, accept the fact that you are creative. Big ideas got you where you are. Do you have a habit of getting some aspect of your business only part of the way to completion, maybe 60 percent of the way, and then you get bored? There are enterprises that rabbit trail from this to that and then onto something else and never fully complete a specific idea. This chapter is about developing a big idea to its full value through a laser beam focus on an identified niche target market.

If you discover yourself, and maybe your enterprise, drifting, consider delegating the completion of an idea to other people who love that aspect of business. Use the resources generated from the older ideas that are being completed by others to fund the new exciting opportunities that keep percolating in your mind.

Accounting systems can be designed to allow for both finishing the old ideas and funding the new ones. Beware of the Freeport folly, which in my opinion exemplified a horrific diversion. Some might also think of the recent Twinkie situation—shenanigans, really, that worked to destroy a major company when management no longer functioned as it should. Some blame workers; some blame the changes in food consumption, but the constant changes in management are another factor.

Continued on next page...

UW My advice to **unsecured workers** is that you must understand in-depth the customers of an entrepreneurial venture. You must especially understand the customers' rationale for buying a company's unique offerings before attending any employment interviews with the company. The very best research resource is often the organization that is providing professional marketing services to them. In order to determine who that organization is, call the company and simply ask. Another method is to go to the web design company that built and runs the site. Ask about their relationship to the company you wish to interview for a job. Ask about how they became acquainted with the organization. The firm that hired the web design company is very likely the marketing agency. The marketing agency will willingly have long conversation with someone interested in their client, they are, after all, in the marketing business. It is their very nature to broadcast about their clients. Data mining takes many forms this is but one of them. Asking the marketing firm about the ultimate customers of the firm you desire to apply to is often very pleasant. The information you gather can then be topics for discussions within the employment interviews.

This is plowing the ground before a seed is planted. Doing economic and financial research before going on interviews demonstrates that you are a different cut of cloth from the standard job seeker. This kind of research is a huge separator from the crowd and important when seeking to work with an entrepreneur.

CHAPTER 6

Entrepreneurial Element Five: Capital Formation

The fifth element of an entrepreneurial mind and, by extension, of an entrepreneurial business, is capital. It's the wherewithal of an organization. Have you ever worked for an organization and had the feeling that you were on an ocean liner only later to find out it was the Titanic? Perhaps you got left in the icy cold water of unemployment and were one of the lucky ones who found a life boat to survive. Sadly, some of us went absolutely down with the ship and filed for bankruptcy along with the organization. That's way too close for comfort for a lot of people.

This chapter is dedicated to the subject of capital formation and deployment for an entrepreneurial organization. The venture requires people trained and skilled in accounting and finance with managerial integration talent. It's not enough to simply be a bean counter. You've got to be a bean counter, yes, but you've got to have managerial capability to integrate the bean count with the organization.

A financial statement, past and present, should tell a true and accurate story of the organization. I've encouraged my students at the University of Denver to do as much research as possible before going on an interview for employment. Organizational transparency is becoming more of a norm in the marketplace and that's a welcome development.

> "A financial statement, past and present, should tell a true and accurate story of the organization."

A number of years ago, Ania Jankowsky, one of the students I mentored, was interviewing at a small organization here in Denver—a magazine. They were looking to hire somebody in the business management section of the publication. Ania was interviewing with the director of the human resources. Ania is a native of Poland and did what I recommended she should do: she asked the human resource director for two years of tax returns and a current financial statement on the company because she wanted to understand the financials of the group. The human resources director said, "This is a private company. Even I don't have access to that kind of information," at which time my student said, "Well, then, you're working for the wrong company."

Now this story is humorous, and maybe, had Ania not been an immigrant, not fully understanding American culture at that point, she might not have made this statement, a faux pas in some people's minds. Obviously, she didn't get the job, but I'm not so sure she was wrong in doing what she did because at the company she's now working for, she's been promoted three times. She works in Paris, France. She fell in love, got married, and is working on a family. She secured the right job and transparency was part of that discussion, faux pas or not.

I think in the days to come, working for organizations that are not financially sound is probably not a good business practice. For workers, it represents the opposite of security. The idea is to secure the right job, which means you want to be connected to the right organization, and financials are part of that, part of knowing that your job will have some longevity to it so that you don't have to start this process all over again.

There are five stages in a company's capitalization.

5 STAGES OF CAPITAL FORMATION

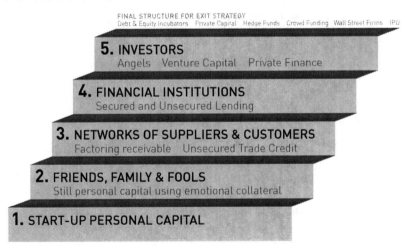

FINAL STRUCTURE FOR EXIT STRATEGY
Debt & Equity Incubators   Private Capital   Hedge Funds   Crowd Funding   Wall Street Firms   IPO

5. INVESTORS
Angels   Venture Capital   Private Finance

4. FINANCIAL INSTITUTIONS
Secured and Unsecured Lending

3. NETWORKS OF SUPPLIERS & CUSTOMERS
Factoring receivable   Unsecured Trade Credit

2. FRIENDS, FAMILY & FOOLS
Still personal capital using emotional collateral

1. START-UP PERSONAL CAPITAL

At the beginning, every company is a start-up. This is Stage 1. You're going to use your own personal capital to start your company. Stage 2 involves friends and families and fools. It's still your own personal company, but the capital is not just your personal capital; it's the company's emotional capital. You're using personal connections as collateral to get your business up and running. Stage 3 is when you're using networks of suppliers and customers to provide creative financing for your business enterprise.

My Denver woodworking guy doesn't pay for most of his wood. They bring in the supplies on a tractor trailer on Monday and he ships out finished goods on the same tractor trailer on Friday. The lumber yard finances all of his raw material because he has a very good business that is very secure for the lumber yard. The lumber-yard management knows they will be paid and they are. That means he has very little of his capital tied up in raw material. In an entrepreneurial business, you can do this as well. The Denver woodworking business is an example of the benefits of supplier networks.

Stage 4 involves financial institutions, when you begin relationships with banks and other outsiders. Loans can be either secured or unsecured. An unsecured loan is one for which you put your signature on the line but you have no capital, no assets to offer as collateral against the loan. A secured loan is one for which you're offering collateral.

Stage 5 is when you build relationships with all outsiders. Here, I'm talking about angel investor groups, venture capital groups, and private capital. This is Wall Street—debt and equity incubators. Ultimately, you may want to become a publicly traded entity for which all of your capital comes from Wall Street investors.

Entrepreneurial businesses can go through every one of the five stages. Each stage has three phases: a beginning, a middle, and an end. Again, the illustrations here will help. The middle phase should be laying the financial foundation for the next stage of capitalization.

Part of every business management process is capital formation—at every stage.

A Blood Test

When I consult with business clients and evaluate their business operations, I commonly review pages and pages of financial information. Spreadsheet extravaganzas!

One of the aspects of this component of my consultancy is to work with the financial departments of the enterprises and/or their outside advisory firms to create a simple, quick assessment tool that is easy to understand yet complete, to quickly determine the health and progress of the organization. Wouldn't it be great to have a financial blood test for a business?

Part of the job of the people who run the capital side of a business is to provide management with that kind of information.

It's an indelible fact that organizations that are exceptionally well managed around elements one through four—that is, they have a big idea, they know who their customers are, they've got great people in the organization, and a laser beam focus—are magnetic to capital. If you tell the story in that context, significant amounts of capital are hunting for great ideas and well-managed companies. That's a universal truth. The issue is being able to put all of that in a package that helps the outsiders—whether bankers, angel investors, or venture capitalists—understand the business. It's more than a business model. It's deeper.

That understanding creates magnetism for capital. It's how you attract the kind of capital you need to keep your company growing. It'll reduce your costs of capital to manage a company this way. Borrowing from credit card companies at eighteen percent is a way of doing business, but boy oh boy, it carries risk and it's expensive. Many of the mainstream companies have been borrowing money at low single digit numbers amortized over six to ten years and that shows you the chasm between capital's lure and its accessibility. Managing your enterprise based on the four elements we have talked about makes the formation of the fifth element much easier.

> "If you're an entrepreneurial leader, do your financial statements support your gut feel for the health of your organization?"

In my experience as a financial advisor and as an economist, there are many operational challenges to managing an entrepreneurial business. I think managing the capital side is one of the most challenging, probably only behind the challenges of managing the people side.

The question is, if you're an entrepreneurial leader, do your financial statements support your gut feel for the health of your organization? I've never sat in front of and spent time with entrepreneurial leaders who didn't, on an internal, visceral level, know whether their company was making progress or not. They don't need to look at a financial statement or a report. They have a sense of how their enterprise is performing—"We're doing really well," or, "Our company is sick." They know that in their gut.

You want to have an accounting and a financial report process that validates what's going on inside. If you feel your company is not healthy, but your financial statements tell you you're paying a lot of income taxes and money is pooling up in your banking accounts, something is wrong. There's a disconnect. The accounting, financial, and capital formation systems of your company should agree with your gut feelings. It's an intuitive aspect of being an entrepreneurial leader, a company health thing.

Do your financial systems clearly validate the progress of your strategy? That is, are they evaluating what it is that you're doing and how well you're doing it? Do they tell you the story? Are you making progress or not? You want to be able to know that quickly. Your system should give you real information quickly. Can you summarize the financial health of your entire enterprise in just a few short pages?

"Produce, within four business days of the close of a calendar month, a report that summarizes everything going on in the business on one page."

I run a full-service financial advisory firm and a broker-dealer with access to the latest Wall Street technology. The financial advisory firm is responsible for managing $175 million in client assets. One of the things we do internally is produce, within four business days of the close of a calendar month, a report that summarizes everything going on in the business on one page. We use the best of technology and systems along with operational and financial expertise to prepare the reports. We live in the capital world and we manage that way. It's the blood test for our business.

Each quarter, the reports take up to thirteen pages. They are quite comprehensive. They are tied to my intuitive sense of the pulse and the health of our business. If the financial reports are validated by what I intuitively think is going on in the business, we continue on, business as usual, full steam ahead.

If the financial statements and the financial reports, the blood tests, tell a different story from the one that I'm feeling in my gut, the analysis is invalid, and I have to go back to diagnose the problem. Either I'm all wet, or there's something wrong with the operations, the client support, the financial accounting, or something else.

What I am saying here will **resonate** with a lot of entrepreneurial people who have an intuitive sense about the health of their business. They have accounting systems designed and built by CPAs and people who are going to report to governing authorities.

What's really necessary, though, from the standpoint of this chapter, is that entrepreneurial companies also have effective managerial accounting. Of course, it's got to be accurate for all the outsiders, the governing entities, and the auditors, and all the other stakeholders. But you need more than that. You need to take what you're doing, everything you're doing, and convert it into something very simple that gives you an idea about the health of your company. And, you've got to be able to do that fast and efficiently.

It's a blood test. I can't tell you how many entrepreneurial companies don't do that. I think it's essential to have such a system because I and many others I know have been able to say, "I personally felt the financial crisis coming in the summer of 2007, almost a year before the financial statements validated and verified the condition."

That statement right there will resonate in the souls of entrepreneurial people. Your company must have a blood test for how it is doing, financially, at any given time. It is something we deal with every day at my company and have worked on for other companies.

I recently did some consulting for a company that raised $2.5 million from angel investors in the private markets. They were ready to go to round 2. They needed to raise another $3 million to bring their company stability and sustainability. They retained our firm to assist with the financial planning necessary to secure round 2.

Keeping in mind the five stages of capitalizing a business, when I did the analysis for them, I said, "You know, you did stage 1, phase 1 capitalization. You skipped stages 2, 3, and 4. Now you're headlong into Stage 5. Because you skipped stages 2, 3, and 4, you'll never get to round 2." They thanked me, wrote me a check, and said, "What do you know? Opinions vary."

I just recently got a note from them that said, "We can't raise any more money. What do we do?" The solution to their capital problem is to retrench financially, go back to the stages they skipped over and transition through them sequentially.

The methodology laid out here will function as a guideline for making progress on the capital formation of a business enterprise.

As a side bar, the company mentioned above filed for liquidation. They were another casualty of ineffective capital formation. Fifty people lost their employment and investors received tax deductions instead of capital gains. Unfortunately, it's a common refrain: jobs and a company gone. Had they only listened to my original advice about the five stages, they might still be here, doing better than surviving, maybe even thriving.

The antidote to their business error is to go back and do phase 2, and then load in phase 3, and they've got to grow more slowly than they had planned. What I want to emphasize is that there is a sequential nature to the way you raise capital and the way you manage your enterprise.

Brace yourselves as this next section is very untraditional. How public are your company's financials? Do you operate as a transparent organization? With the exception of specific payroll and sensitive competitive data, can any employee or potential customer review the financial status of the company in which they work or with which they are contemplating building a business relationship? Should they be able to? What kind of culture would be created if every worker could have a complete understanding of the financial results of their efforts on behalf of their company? With employee loyalty to corporate America waning, can entrepreneurial organizations continue to operate on the basis of a simple "trust me?" At Destiny Capital we operate on high levels of trust and our transparent management—even when it doesn't have to be transparent—demonstrates the trustworthiness of our organization. Trust but verify.

The application of that mantra to an unsecured worker means not working blind in an organization. The story that I told earlier about my student Ania is an example. She didn't get the job, but maybe it was the wrong job anyway. Maybe it was a job that she wouldn't have wanted. Who's to know? The old idea of trust but verify—I think that's where we're headed.

If you're an unsecured worker, don't you really want to be part of an organization where you're making a contribution to the betterment of the organization? Don't you want to be in a place where what you do matters and what you do counts? Of course! You want to be able to see the progress of your organization and your role in it. That's a whole different reward system, which doesn't have anything to do with money, but it has everything to do with emotional rewards.

> "That's a whole different reward system, which doesn't have anything to do with money, but it has everything to do with emotional rewards."

I manage an organization in an industry that just experienced a huge downturn. A large percentage of my competitors have gone out of business over the last five years. They're done. How would you like to be an employee who worked really hard for four years in an organization that ended up not surviving? That's just emotionally devastating. Being in an organization that's transparent, where you can have a complete line of sight—"I'm adding to the productivity and the advantage of this organization"—is a positive motivator for your human resource and the health of your company. It also adds clarity to an organization that is struggling financially. Sometimes the solution to company problems comes from the rank and file, not the owners. Could giving the workers information about the organization be part of solving the problems encountered?

If you are trying to secure the right job, let me suggest that the right job is one with an organization you can hook on to and go north (make progress), as an individual and also as a member of the collective, the organization.

Another point I want to make is that sometimes people get hung up on being the next Steve Jobs or the next Mary Kay Ash. You can have small niche ideas that do really well, smart ideas that inspire somebody to say, "Why didn't I think of that?" and they can be the littlest thing you can think of.

The last of the five points in this chapter is that you don't have to strive to be a publicly traded company to do this stuff. For example, I'm a private company. I'm a Wall Street company, but all of our financial information is posted on our website for review by current customers, prospective customers, and everybody on my staff because I think the days of clouded-in-mysticism financial advisors are done. I believe that time period should be over.

I think the whole idea of privacy in the days of the Internet is history. It's done, it's over. If you're operating in an untoward manner, you're going to be found out. I'm absolutely convinced. Hiding is long gone. Just the idea of privacy is kind of laughable. If you don't believe that, Google yourself and go to Ancestors.com, and find out all kinds of stuff about your family tree and lineage. I think that'll also translate into your financials as well.

EL For the **entrepreneurial leader**, effective management is a marketing advantage. The capital formation and financial planning of an entrepreneurial organization is the magnetism holding all of the moving parts of the enterprise together.

Think of chemistry in which the central nucleus of an atom is composed of protons and neutrons. Their magnetism keeps the electrons spinning in a stable, continuous, and perpetual orbit. That's how finance should be, not rigid but rather flexible, alive, and magnetic. Do you, as an entrepreneurial leader, get a financial blood test for your business within a short period of time after the close of all accounting periods?

Is your accounting a living, breathing, dynamic part of your entrepreneurial organization? How would you know if your company was sick? Does your financial information tell a story that's congruent with what your intuition is telling you about your company? Describe your relationship with the stakeholders of your entrepreneurial business. How comfortable are you with being financially transparent with them?

UW As an **unsecured worker** considering a company as a potential work site, part of your data mining has to be financial. Can you get current and historic financial information? Securing the right job has to include some analysis of the organization's current and historic financial capabilities.

CHAPTER 7

Entrepreneurial Element Six: Coordinated Orchestration

T his is the sixth element in the mindset of an entrepreneur, somebody who can take all of the other five elements and knit them
together in a way that makes rational sense. To demonstrate a
very effective example of how entrepreneurs are wired, I'm going to
take a little bit of a diversion here.

My middle son is a musician. A number of years ago he gave a recital in which he performed a solo in front of his peers, and the audience also included a group of professors. I can't think of anything that would be more stressful than that. When he finished that performance, one of the questions that I asked him was, "What's harder to do, a solo performance like that or playing in the orchestra?" He told me, without hesitation, that playing in the orchestra was harder. I gave him that tilt of the head, an I-don't-understand-what-you-just-told-me look, and he replied, "When I'm doing a solo, all I have to do is play. All I have to do is go to that deep center of me and let it come forth. I don't have to think about anything other than what my passion is in playing a particular piece of music. Dad, that's as close as I'm going to get to heaven without dying." I just loved that.

> **"In our culture, linear thinking detracts from business management."**

It was my son's further explanation about the orchestra that really struck me. He said, "When I'm in the orchestra, I can't do that. I have to play my instrument to the best of my ability, but I have to listen to the other people in my section. I have to listen to the other clarinets in my unit. I have to pay attention to what the French horns are doing and the beat of the bass and the percussionists and all of the other pieces of the music and the notes that they are playing. Then I have to listen for blending in, because the idea is to make beautiful music together. Then I have to pay attention to the conductor who is really the orchestra leader in making sure that the music we're making is a performance that is pleasing to the audience. That's why the orchestra is so much harder rather than a solo."

This fits with elements of an entrepreneurial mind, the idea of the entrepreneurial leader as the conductor of an orchestra in that it's infinitely harder to take all of the other five elements and blend them together in a way that is pleasing and beautiful. We all know what it can be like to sit in the audience at a concert and listen to really bad music. We might be thinking, "That was excruciating. I can't believe I paid my money to hear that." You also know the other side of that: "Oh my gosh, that's just the best I've ever heard." You can translate that to business as well.

In our culture, linear thinking detracts from business management. This is because business management is circular. Most orchestras are set up almost in a semicircle. That's partly why music is such a powerful metaphor for people; it operates on circular thinking; it has a circular impact.

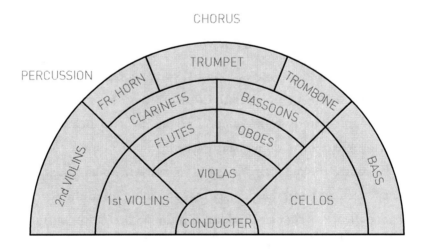

Businesses that operate on circular thinking progress to effective synergy, working together faster. They reach synergy more quickly. It's an art. You could read a thousand business management books and still miss the art of effectively tying a business organization to-

"You could read a thousand business management books and still miss the art of effectively tying a business organization together because it's not a science; it's an art."

gether because it's not a science; it's an art.

If you're the entrepreneurial leader, you've got to be able to take your big idea and blend it with the customers that will benefit from it. You've got to find great people who also are captivated with the big idea and customer orientation. You need to be able to coordinate them in such a way that they have a laser beam focus on what it is that you're trying to accomplish so everybody is on board and moving in the same direction.

You've got to do your economics; you've got to do your finance. You've got to be able to operate in such a way that you're running a sustainable enterprise in which everyone benefits financially as a result of what you're doing, starting with the customers and working backward to your staff. You need to continue to pay attention to the environment and the changes that are going on in the economy. That's part of the circular thinking and the orchestration of running and managing a business.

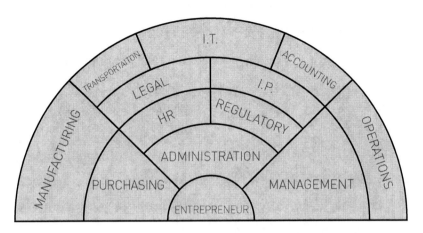

MARKETING & SALES

Entrepreneurial leaders in this sector think about technology and technology integrators as acceleration points for business. They're often thinking about how technology can help their company get better, get faster, improve the quality of what they do. If you do what you've always done, and not make use of technology, you're going to get what you've always gotten. This is a reworded version of the definition of insanity. If you do what you have always done and expect a different result, then you are insane. In business if you do what you have always done and don't change you are going to get what you always got, which is behind.

Technology is the great leveler and the great accelerator and a good entrepreneurial business is going to want to know how to work with it. I can hardly think of any kind of business today that, when fully integrating technology processes into its business, doesn't get better.

As an entrepreneurial leader, you're also going to think about your business methods and your processes. Are my organizational skills, my organizational processes as efficient as they can be? Is there something that we should change? You're looking for continuous improvements because regardless of how good you are, you want to get better. You also want to be able to see the freight train coming, the critical business-impacting factor that no one sees.

You want to have great people in your organization who have the freedom to speak up: "I see a problem coming here and we should be able to think about it ahead of time and navigate through it." Some of that is going to come from your rank-and-file employees who are empowered to think and operate and make a difference in the enterprise.

> "As an entrepreneurial leader, sometimes you'll understand where your business is going, but sometimes you don't necessarily communicate that very well to the people who are in the boat, rowing."

Coordination also means you're thinking about coordinating your accounting systems. You think about accounting systems, surely, because you want to report to all the externals, the regulators, the compliance people. You live in an environment where you get to pay taxes, and accounting is designed to figure out how much money you made, and how much the government gets, and so on.

Also, an entrepreneur wants an accounting system that helps him or her make managerial decisions. We touched on it a little bit in the last chapter when we talked about an accounting process that operates like a blood test, telling you right away whether you're healthy and getting healthier or whether you're sick and getting sicker. It's a really critical thing. It's an addition to the way you do traditional profit and loss, balance sheets, and accounting processes.

Coordination also means thinking about your legal framework, the legal containers for your intellectual property and your ownership structures—in other words, a description of who owns what. What kind of an organization do you have, a sole proprietorship or a partnership? If it's a corporation, what kind of corporation is it? Maybe your enterprise should be a limited liability company or a limited liability partnership. Somebody in the organization is going to need to make a decision regarding the best legal framework for your business to thrive. If your company does international business, determining who can assist your enterprise through the maze of international laws and regulations in each different jurisdiction in which you do business is critical. It's the decision of the entrepreneurial leader to select the right person to manage this aspect of the business.

Coordination also means managing your marketing and sales people, your direct contacts who have a laser beam focus on customers, who I refer to as the outside world. Your sales and marketing people are closest to the customers themselves. They may have closer relationships with the customers than the manufacturing or operations departments have. What are they telling you about what's happening in the marketplace? You have to manage your marketing and sales divisions.

The element of coordination is the one that reduces the report on your business operation to ten pages maximum so that you can present it to your business stakeholders. It's about communicating how your business is doing to the people who are working inside it. As an entrepreneurial leader, sometimes you'll understand where your business is going, but sometimes you don't necessarily communicate that very well to the people who are in the boat, rowing.

A good entrepreneurial business manager is going to bring every element of his or her business together so that all are on board; they're all moving in the same direction, and they understand where they are, where they're headed, and how their contribution matters. Element six is the ultimate skill of orchestration.

The embodiment of the sixth element of an entrepreneurial mind is somebody who can tie all the pieces together and simplify them to provide a communication device for everybody who works in the organization. Ultimately, your business needs to function collectively in order to maximize synergy, which comes down to productivity and profits. A good entrepreneurial leader will have the ability to keep everybody working on the same page.

One book I highly recommend is the bestselling *Good to Great: Why Some Companies Make the Leap...and Others Don't*, which was written in 2001 by Jim Collins. One of the concepts that he talks about in his book is the flywheel. The flywheel means that all of the people in the business organization are working together, pushing the elements of the business forward perpetually and in the same direction. The flywheel concept is one of the things that keeps the business from doing rabbit trails and getting diversified to the point where the company is not productive. It's a great leveler of businesses, preventing them from being bureaucratic rather than productive.

This element of an entrepreneurial mind requires circular thinking rather than linear and it requires the ultimate in team building and sharing: communication—rapidly communicating information system wide, so people in your organization have the facts.

One of the big technological accelerators in this area is the intranet—a communications system people can log into 24/7, giving them access to important business information that they need for their jobs and that affects the entire organization. With an intranet system, everybody knows exactly where the company is at any given time. That's part of the sixth element of tying stuff together.

Acting as a member of a team takes a lot more effort than acting as an individual. When you are an entrepreneur, your goal is to be a big visionary thinker, which sometimes affects your ability to work well with other people. Teamwork is harder because you have to make sure everybody synchronizes well.

You can carry that illustration a little bit further in that orchestras are organized around a series of strategic work teams. You have your percussion, you have your string section—all the different orchestral sections have to work together synergistically to form a smoothly functioning whole. If the conductor is the entrepreneur, the employee is the soloist or the orchestra itself.

Many of the great visionaries know that they need a balance, someone to orchestrate, someone to help them with their businesses. Strong personalities, which are typical of entrepreneurial leaders, need to be counterbalanced. They need operations help. They need people skills. They need sales. They've got to be able to share and coordinate. If you're Mr. Hyde, it's good you've got Dr. Jekyll running your organization, somebody who counterbalances your personality. I have already told you about Pat Kramer with my company.

The best example I can give you is that of a famous company: Mark Zuckerberg's Facebook. Even back in Harvard, when he founded Facebook as merely a college social project, he knew he would need people around him. Zuckerberg did not have deep social skills, and he found those in his roommate Chris Hughes, who became the company's first spokesperson, the one Zuckerberg relied on to answer e-mails and questions. There is no doubt that Mark Zuckerberg is a genius, and he

"Many of the great visionaries know that they need a balance, someone to orchestrate, someone to help them with their businesses. Strong personalities, which are typical of entrepreneurial leaders, need to be counterbalanced.

profoundly changed the Internet as we know it today. As of this writing, more than one billion people have Facebook profiles. Yet even Zuckerberg knew he needed help, he needed someone to counterbalance his nerdy computer-genius ways. He found it through Chris Hughes and many others he had in his circle in his early days.

True entrepreneurial spirit is manifest in the founding of Facebook and in Zuckerberg who recognized his own shortcomings and found the right people to counterbalance them. Most of those early people, Chris Hughes among them, are profoundly wealthy. Zuckerberg, we know, is worth billions. Yes, these are extreme examples and few entrepreneurs or their inner circle will become so wealthy, but it gives you an idea of the kind of thinking behind this book, both for entrepreneurs and for those who will be working for and with them.

I might add that this is also the era of the dot com. The first Internet boom, in the late 1990s, mostly led to the first Internet bust. Many entrepreneurs established companies, but many were more interested in flash and spectacle, IPOs, and being on the scene and in gossip magazines. Many did not surround themselves with the right people. You need to be more than just a genius with bright ideas. You need to have public relations people, people who make good financial decisions, good accountants, good people keeping an eye on the money—people balancing out your own skills as an entrepreneur.

Managerial decision making is important in any new company, in any start-up. It's not just about profit and loss statements and balance sheets. It's about an accounting system that is very much like blood tests, telling you whether your company is healthy and getting healthier or if it's sick and getting sicker.

For me, living and breathing in the world of capital, that's one of the things on which I counsel all of my small companies. If you don't have the ability or a process to get a blood test on your company really quickly, you need one. You've got to figure out whether your business is where it should be. That means accountants really need to do a better job of not just counting the beans, but also interpreting what they mean. That interpretation process is managerial accounting. You've got to build your systems for that. And that is where hiring the right people is important, as is being able to project yourself, if you're a job seeker, as the right person for such a position, as someone who will complement your entrepreneur boss.

Through my work, I have found many entrepreneurs don't necessarily think about those nuts and bolts of running their companies. This book is targeted at some of those entrepreneurs whose businesses just aren't operating the way they woulda, coulda, shoulda. They're not growing in the manner they would like. Do you have the right people surrounding you? This should be an aha moment for you men and women out there, saying to yourselves, "Hmm, I never thought of that."

I also think those of you who are in the job market must stress your skills in interviews and how they complement what the entrepreneur is trying to achieve. That way both the entrepreneur and the employee can grow. You might not become Zuckerberg or Hughes, but there's nothing wrong with that as a goal.

EL Being able to work with all five elements of the entrepreneurial mind—the big idea, the customer orientation, the marvelous people who chose to work here at Destiny Capital, the laser beam focus of our enterprise, and finally, managing our capital—is my ultimate task as a manager. I often feel that it would be wonderful if I were an octopus with multiple tentacles to tend to each of these business aspects as well as do the forty to fifty hours of "regular" everyday work. But it is the life I have chosen. This coordination of all five elements simply comes with the territory. My deepest hope is that this book will give you a pattern to follow that will allow mere mortals, and not only those with octopus-like tentacles, to perform well. This chapter is dedicated to pulling it all together. Don't get scared and squirt ink all over.

UW For those of you who are **unsecured workers,** there is much I want you to think about in this chapter. For the last decade, as I have worked with my students at Denver University, I have coached them on "feeling" an organization. A group that operates poorly in the sixth element of coordination feels disorganized and sometimes frantic. The opposite is true for well-managed organizations. During the interviewing process, pay attention to the linkages between the five elements described in the previous chapters. Does this organization exhibit the characteristic traits of a well-run company? When you toured the company, did it look and feel comfortably managed? When interviewing the other team members, were they, on balance, happy and engaged? Look for demonstrated clues to the quality of management in this critical area of coordination. In a sentence, do they make beautiful music together as a company? Please read (or go back and reread) the opening of this chapter to fully understand what I mean.

CHAPTER 8

It Actually Does Take a Hero

The conductor has a very difficult job. In the illustrations, that role is fulfilled by the entrepreneurial owner. Even though most conductors are in their own right excellent musicians, when standing in front of an orchestra, they are not playing an instrument; they are leading. Leading is hard work. The conductor encourages each musician, each section, to perform as a member of a team. The conductor's leadership skills make the difference between a good and exceptional performance.

The illustration on the following page is from the orientation manual we use here at Destiny Capital. The entire presentation is in the appendix of this book and is available in a PowerPoint format. Simply contact us and we will e-mail it to you. (Our contact information is on page 131.) This orientation presentation is used to help new employees understand how we function as a company. It is the central point of our company culture, which is, professionally, patient. We are a functional, family-style, close-knit group by design.

It Doesn't Take a Hero

H. Norman Schwarzkopf (1934–2012) was the commanding general in the US Army during the Desert Shield and Desert Storm campaigns of 1990 and 1991. In 1992 he wrote his autobiography, *It Doesn't Take a Hero*. It is centrally placed in the Musick library, thoroughly marked up and highlighted, just like all the others books on those shelves. I made his book mine. I synthesized six principles of leadership from his pages. Mind you, he never wrote an isolated chapter like this one, but rather, laced his leadership principles throughout the text. Since he was a national military hero commanding troops in horrific conditions, his leadership style had credibility. While we are not fighting in an armed conflict—at least, that is the case with most of us—it sure seems as if we have been in a battle or two over the years. Gazing across the titles just now—I am writing this from my office, the "Womb Room"—I must have ten books by eight different authors on the subject of leadership. Schwarzkopf's gets the central location because his book and the leadership principles that come from it were actually demonstrated and tested in a world where talk is cheap but true action carries the day. In a world where theory is as prevalent as practice, I favor practical action when adopting a leadership style.

7 PRINCIPLES OF LEADERSHIP

It is our heartfelt determined desire to do personally what we expect of all team members of our firm.

1. All people should be fully equipped, ready to serve every day.

2. Take care of our team members *and* their families by:
   1. including all family members on our regular special events
   2. being truly interested in more than *just* business productivity!

3. Encourage and model loyalty to one another.

4. Teach by example in thought, word and deed.

5. *Never* pass by a mistake. View it as an opportunity for learning.

6. Do what is *right! Always!*

7. Communicate openly, directly, honestly and freely toward each other and toward management.

Leadership principle number one is demonstrated continuously throughout our firm. Recently I attended an in-service provided by our law firm on a variety of subjects. One of the topics was how to navigate the recent legislative amendment to the Colorado Constitution legalizing marijuana. I thought about amendments to company policy manuals and the codification of the company liability insurance policies recommended by the lawyers. Principle number one takes care of all that without the need to institute new manuals or insure for the risk. We do have an up-to-date, two-inch thick, employee manual, but never in 37 years have we had a problem with any kind of substance abuse. This principle is also why we routinely decommission our computer technology every three years to upgrade our systems to the very best in class, because everyone should be equipped and ready to serve every day. Finally, it is also through this principle that we encourage people, if they are sick, to stay home and get well. We would prefer they not drag themselves into work, lengthening their illness and probably infecting the rest of us and the clients who come in for services. Take care of yourselves. The work will be here whenever you can return.

Principle number two is practical action because we see our entire staff as whole people rather than simply units of production capability. A new person on staff had been working with us for a few months when she called early one morning, leaving a voice message, text and an e-mail. She had been up all night with her daughter. She made a decision to take her to the local clinic early but was likely going to be in late. She called again at 7:30 a.m. to say the clinic was backed up and she was going to be later than she first thought. At 9:30 a.m. she called and said that someone from her family was able to arrange the work schedule to be with her daughter. She would be in ASAP. When she finally arrived, she looked like someone who had been up all night and under no small amount of stress.

I was about to add to it. I sat down with her and said, "Samantha your behavior was totally inappropriate." She visibly shook when those words hit her ear drums. She started to get a little bit misty. I continued, leaning in to her space from across the desk—keep in mind she had just been through new employee orientation two months previously. "We see you as wife and mother first and a worker here as a distant second. One communication would have been sufficient. You will get here when you get here; it's okay. Now I want you to think about where you should be right now. If it's with your daughter, then go be with her. If she is covered and you are wanting to get in a full day's work, then drink up; we can start. A week later she asked if she could see me privately. She apologized for her behavior. Over her career she has read lots of orientation manuals written by lawyers and HR compliance people. Never had she been involved with a company that *actually followed* what was written in them. I can imagine H. Norman Schwarzkopf now in his celestial clothing grinning over that comment.

Principle number three was demonstrated recently when another one of our staff members, La Rae Heinle, fell in her garage and broke the ankle bones of her left leg (ouch.) She was unable to come to work for six weeks. Our staff and management team reorganized their workloads to accommodate the added duties while she was away. Once she returned, she was not at full speed, so we all pitched in to lighten her load as she needed rehab and lots of physical therapy. We have sick leave and paid-time-off policies allowing all staff members to accumulate paid time off as they work. La Rae had burned through her entire accrued balance. Several staff members asked management if they could donate vacation and sick leave days so she and Alan could get away during the summer for a vacation—a practical demonstration of loyalty among coworkers.

> " Effective leadership is the prow of the ice breaker busting through the thick sea ice, creating a navigable water way in its wake. Is your organization a seaworthy vessel?

Principles four, five, and six are a continuous activity. Effective leadership is the prow of the ice breaker busting through the thick sea ice, creating a navigable water way in its wake. Is your organization a seaworthy vessel?

The seventh principle was not synthesized from H. Norman, but is of my own creation because of a particular quirk of mine. I try to be sensitive to the needs and circumstances of my entire staff, but unfortunately, I have two strikes against me to start with. I am an entrepreneur and I am a male. I do not take hints. A number of years ago one of our workers was pregnant and there were activities women do to celebrate such events.

Since we were traditionally left out of the loops on the baby showers, we invented the testosterone version, just for guys. Each male employee and spouse of a female employee was invited to the Musick home for a poker shower. They were asked to bring a bunch of money and something to drink. We played cards with the winner taking the final prize. At the end of the night, the winner would donate the final pot to the father to be.

A few days after the first shower, one of our female staff members appeared to be upset. Finally, I cut through the iceberg that had grown between us and asked straight out what was wrong. "My husband lost a fair amount of money at the poker shower the other night. He was unaware the total final pot was to go to the father to be." Most of us had taken it in our stride as a part of the celebration. Well, her husband was not happy, so neither was she. So, here's principle number seven: If somebody loses a chunk of money at the next poker shower and the employee gets upset, or if the employee is upset for any reason at all, he or she is empowered and encouraged to come directly to me and clear the air. No hinting please! And I promise to get better at reading between the lines.

Those leadership principles written by a serious man for serious events in history are demonstrated every day as we manage our entrepreneurial enterprise. I believe we continue the legacy of the actual hero who wrote the book. I would like to say a thank you to H. Norman, believing he is worthy to receive the honor of a hero for his leadership. I also believe he smiles from heaven when he sees people in the here and now, living life the way he did. I was very sad the day they laid him to rest, February 28, 2013, at West Point.

Directional Dozen: How We Work As One
Three Foundation Essentials

Mission

Vision

Core Values

Mission: Managing family wealth for generations

Vision: To be a company that courageously cares for people

Core Values:

1. Integrity assured through transparency;
   no hidden conflicts of interest;

2. Patience because haste brings poverty;

3. Dedication through cooperative effort; clients
   do their part (providing time and information);
   we do our part to serve them.

The Necessary Nine

Just as scaffolding and the girding supported the reconstruction of the Statue of Liberty, so does the Necessary Nine support our mission, vision, and core values:

9. Organizational development

8. Team building

7. Leadership

6. Teaching gifts

5. Management

4. Experience

3. Education and training

2. Talent

1. Effort

Components 1 and 2 are both components of raw material required to be part of the Destiny team.

1. **Effort:** making a personal decision to desire a positive outcome

2. **Talent:** ability and aptitude, capacity to learn new things, and God-given fundamental foundation ability

Components 3 and 4 are both elements of the refinery process for components 1 and 2.

3. **Education:** the continuous acquisition of knowledge through formal courses and practical experimentation for use in real life; training: the continuous, hands-on, interactive, specific information and coaching to improve performance in real life;

4. **Experience:** the combination of training and education multiplied by (not simply added to) application in real life.

The *continuous* process of refining component 1 (effort) and component 2 (talent) through the use of components 3 (education and training) and 4 (experience) enables every team member the opportunity to obtain exceptional career opportunities.

Management: the daily process of focusing all the aspects of our firm: the three foundational essentials combine with the first four of The Necessary Nine components, to create an environment that facilitates individual growth *and* team building.

Teaching gifts: The ability to assist people to combine: 1 (effort) and 2 (talent) with 3 (education and training) and 4 (experience) to produce quality results at an accelerated rate.

It is our heartfelt desire to do ourselves what we expect of all our team members.

Seven Principles of Leadership

1. All people should be fully equipped and ready to serve every day.

2. We take care of our team members *and* their families by 1) including all family members on our regular special events, and 2) being truly interested in more than *just* business productivity!

3. We encourage and model loyalty to one another.

4. We teach by example in thought, word, and deed.

5. We *never* pass by a mistake. We view it as an opportunity for learning.

6. We do what is *right. Always!*

7. We communicate openly, directly, honestly, and freely with each other and management.

8. We build teams: We have the ability and the desire to synergize with coworkers for the benefit of our clients and, as a result, benefit ourselves—*in that order.* No Lone Rangers exist in our firm. There will *never* be room for them in the future.

9. We foster organizational development. We strive to become an organization that has the ability to reach high to grasp the destiny that has been set before us, to make a positive difference in every challenge

we encounter together, and to improve the financial health of each client we are privileged to serve.

The reconstruction of the Statue of Liberty was ultimately completed. The supportive structures were removed to reveal the refurbished work. We see that the work of management, however, is never done. We all are perpetually under construction and therefore our enterprise, unlike the real Statue of Liberty, will forever have the scaffolding and girding of The Necessary Nine to support the three foundational essentials of mission, vision, and core values.

The three foundational essentials that bring forth liberty, supported by the scaffolding and girding of the management structure for continuous improvements under construction—this is the management style of Destiny Capital.

EL

When was the last time you, as an **entrepreneurial leader**, had your leadership style assessed? You can hire a management consultant to be evaluated with a detailed report. It happens all the time. But there is a better way. Try the 360-degree performance evaluation. Does your organization employ full performance reviews? By full I mean do those who are supervised have the opportunity to write performance evaluations on the leaders? Many times performance evaluations simply operate one way. Leaders and managers evaluate the performance of their direct reports. Do the direct reports have the opportunity to write reviews of their managers in their upline? Amazing learning on leadership style can be obtained by having 360 evaluations. It takes character and a strong dose of humility to subject yourself, as an entrepreneurial leader, to reviews by people for whom you are responsible. They will, in a high trust culture (which is created when the six entrepreneurial elements are put into practice), give you feedback that will help you and the entire organization improve. How else do you think I know that I am difficult to work around at times and am not good at taking hints? **I have trained my staff to be brutally honest in their 360-degree evaluations of me.** The corollary to that is that my staff members are also subject to the same 360 evaluation. It's a fabulous tool. I use it in my class at the university, having students evaluate (yes that means grading) one another every week. I am training them for a high trust culture in the organizations that will dominate job generation from 2013 through 2033. They will be used to 360 evaluations even before they arrive in business and industry. The students destined to start their own businesses will be 360ers right from the start. Want to be a hero to your organization? Then read the chapter, mark it up in the margins, and create your own leadership manual for existing employees to read and new employees to devour. Then live it daily.

Continued on next page...

UW

Unsecured workers—okay, in this chapter the gloves come off— should know that in entrepreneurial organizations, *everyone* leads. People will have different responsibilities, but everyone takes initiative. It's a normal method of operating. Years ago I had giraffes made for every staff member and bought ceramic giraffe figurines that were placed all over the office. They are still there. I detected a slight sense of hesitancy within our group. Rather than address the negative emotion, fear—by the way, it's easy in a financial advisory firm to get frightened from time to time because it is a large ocean out there and we are but a small ship and this was after the Enron collapse, after all—I chose to accentuate the positive in that I wanted all members of our staff to stick their necks out, become giraffes, not turtles. Our culture at Destiny Capital makes it safe to take emotional risks. When you interview with organizations, are the existing employees giraffes or turtles? Think about it. Read this chapter like a leader because you are going to have to be in order to work effectively in small and medium-sized businesses.

CHAPTER 9

Success Measures

An organization effectively orchestrated can produce movement. Can you feel the movement of your organization? Does that match up with what the company's financial statements are showing? Is your company moving at the best pace to allow for sustainable cash flow? Management can produce movement in two specific areas: margin expansion and marketing receptivity.

In Chapter 2, I introduced two managerial concepts using two different stories. The first one was about Disney and theme park design. Disney is exceptional for moving people emotionally. The line illustration below describes the transitional process a customer encounters as he or she experiences a product or a service. The left side is PAIN. The right side is PLEASURE. In order to generate marketing movement, a business enterprise will design its offerings to either relieve pain or induce pleasure. The organization that can create the greatest movement in their customers along that line will have opportunities to become a successful company. When our family gets together during holidays, we still tell stories about our Disney vacations, including the sound of the music and the smells enjoyed while floating over the orange groves on the Soarin' flight simulator ride. It is a powerful memory that has staying power. Disney is a master at generating marketing movement.

Not every company can be a Disney. But within your existing enterprise, how can you create movement along this pain-to-pleasure line? What can you do to increase the wow factor of your product or service? Perhaps you can engage a marketing service to look from the outside to the inside and help you see aspects of your organization that have been hidden from your day-to-day vision of the business. In a moment of courage, ask your existing staff for their ideas about movement along this line. Finally, survey existing customers on why they work with you and what keeps them coming back. Ask if there is something they would like you to do to enhance the experience of doing business with them.

The second story in this book was about turning trash into treasure. Bob Corn, the owner of Arvada Appliance, used to buy used machines for $5, rehab them, and sell them for $35. That was back in 1968. Today they use the same business strategy of trash into treasure, now accelerated by Internet surfing sites such as Craigslist, continuously looking to add to their inventory of old machines. This business strategy can be illustrated with a vertical line. Trash is the point at the bottom with treasure at the top. The greater the distance between two points on this line, the greater the chance a business has to become a manageable. Businesses with wide margins have wonderful chances to become sustainable enterprises.

If the answers to the questions posed at the beginning of this chapter were either "no" or "I don't know," now would be a good time to open up the diagnostics and determine the reason for the lack of necessary performance. Work together with your teams to diagnose the problems and work together for a solution. Take the opportunity to move the company north by improving margins. Look for long-term solutions to margin expansion. It is relatively easy to cut expenses in order to meet a short-term milestone. It is quite another to look for changes that meet current goals while at the same time building increased potential for continuous and regular gain sharing for all members of the staff.

The title of this book is *The Job Generation*. I am on a mission to do what I can to put America back to work again. Creating new entrepreneurial businesses and energizing existing ones will create

> **I am on a mission to do what I can to put America back to work again."**

employment. I love teaching and training this new generation of workers how to understand the six elements of an entrepreneurial mind. It will help them secure the right jobs in the small and mid-sized business segment. This is my opportunity to fix what is broken in our current job markets and economic culture.

So now we put the last two concepts of business movement together:

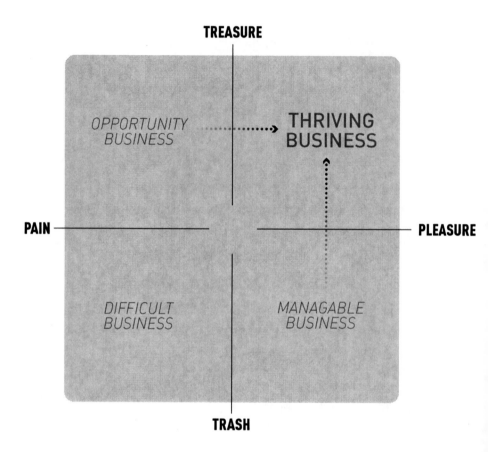

The trash-to-treasure-and-pain-to-pleasure system organized on the previous page creates four distinct zones of business operation.

The lower left quadrant is a very difficult business, likely one in serious need of an overhaul. A business having wide margins but weak movement on the pain-pleasure axis is an opportunity business. This kind of company has an opportunity to become sustainable with better impact of goods and services on customers.

The lower right quadrant is a manageable business that can become an effective organization through improving margins. Now, opportunity businesses and manageable businesses have carried on for decades on the power of the current economic system of capitalism that governs America. The suggestion here is to pay attention to movement on both the horizontal and vertical planes.

"Large companies are not the largest employers in America."

The remaining quadrant is reserved for great companies. They are thriving businesses. A management team charged with the task of orchestrating and leading an organization to become a thriving business concentrates continuously on moving the organization up and to the right. The Fortune 500 index is full of companies in this quadrant. It's how they managed to become part of that publically traded index of large companies. But large companies are not the largest employers in America. It's the small businesses that employ the lion's share of the work force. Manageable businesses work to increase margins. Opportunity businesses look for ways to increase their "footprint" within the marketplace and within their industry.

If more businesses can move themselves into the thriving category, our country will change for the better. Job generation will become a reality both as a verb and as a noun. We can, in fact, become an economy that creates millions of new jobs. It could also become the next demographic cohort, joining the baby boomers, generation

X, and the millennials in the dictionaries of social scientists. The job generation—I kind of like the sound of that, don't you?

Here is my final thought for this chapter: the challenge ahead is daunting. For a visual reference, place this book (or your Kindle or Nook) flat on the surface of the place where you are sitting. Lift the last illustration by the right upper corner. The movement arrows on the paper now point uphill. The degree of incline just became steeper. American companies, especially small businesses, fight a continuous battle similar to gravity. These forces continue to push businesses into the lower left quadrant. Sometimes it takes tremendous effort to simply maintain the current position against the omnipresent adversary of gravity. I understand. I live in this country too. However, I still believe resources to generate movement sufficient to overcome the wear and tear of gravity are within reach of businesses today. Creating movement sufficient to climb into the thriving business quadrant is still clearly within our national reach. I guess it is not hard to detect the trapper/trader, mountain-man, entrepreneurial DNA I inherited from my ancestors who made Colorado home in the 1850s.

"Creating movement sufficient to climb into the thriving business quadrant is still clearly within our national reach."

APPLICATIONS & TAKEAWAYS

EL Every organization is moving somewhere continually. How do you, as the **entrepreneurial leader,** generate movement in your organization? The pages here show two methods that, when applied together, help organizations make progress. In difficult times, like the last decade, these companies survived and perhaps grew marginally. When environments change for better, these organizations thrive. Moving from opportunity businesses and manageable businesses to thriving businesses will bring job generation to our country and increasing capital to the organization.

UW **Unsecured workers**: when you research organizations to join, do a regression analysis. Get the historical data on where the organization has come from and use that work to determine where the organization is going. See if you can understand if the business is a trash-to-treasure business or one that emotionally moves its customers. Hint: a company that does both well is one worth doing extra work diligently to secure a job. These companies almost never post job availability on bulletin boards, either internal or external. You won't find them on bulletin boards. You have to use your skills of creative detective work and hunt down all the clues to find the thriving organizations within your own communities. Then you want to take the knowledge from this book and package yourself to put yourself in the best light to obtain a job at one of them. Think of it as though you were your own talent agent and you are "selling" yourself to an organization that doesn't even know it needs your collection of skills and talents...yet. It is the ultimate in competition.

CHAPTER 10

The Next Megatrend in American Business

I have referred to the next megatrend in American business earlier in this book. As I field-tested this material at the University of Denver, in my own entrepreneurial enterprise, Destiny Capital, among the current and new clients we serve, and in the marketplace in general, I am convinced the next big move will come from small and mid-sized organizations that are entrepreneurially managed.

The economist in me regards the last so-called lost decade as one of pent-up demand. There have been a great many organizations operating with great hesitation, an almost strategic pause—waiting. I believe the waiting is giving way to the beginning phase of filling up the pent-up demand. In addition, many of the unknowns of our recent past are now becoming known with reasonably predictable outcomes. These outcomes lend themselves to the analytical processes of probability extrapolation, which can be econometrically formulated with dynamic models that have been built and tested.

Our organization produces a blog twice monthly about encouraging economics for everyone. Here is the text for the post of January 16, 2013:

"Slow, Slow, Think Small"

Coming out of the fog of medically induced anesthesia, I heard the nurse say, "We thought we lost you back there." Back there was three weeks prior, in April 1976. The dedicated physical rehabilitation therapists continued a daily refrain saying, "slow, slow, think small." Relearning basic tasks took weeks. The progress was slow, slow, and I had to think in small progress milestones. I did not know then it would take ten years to fully recover. Discipline is built under such circumstances. I continue to apply to the present lessons learned long ago. I often think back to those military days and wonder what purpose was served during that time in my young life. I was nineteen. It occurred to me during the closing days of 2012 that our nation was exiting a long period of uncertainty. Could it be the next period would be a slow-slow-think-small one as well? I believe we are in just such a time.

At my financial advisory firm we believe it is time to revisit old financial architecture because of four recent events that combine to bring about a period of financial and economic rehabilitation. This rehabilitation will likely be characterized by slow, slow progress, gradual improvements over time.

Event one was the fiscal cliff, which really wasn't one.

Event two was the results of elections in the United States, Japan, and China. Political stability and consistent leadership is now set for a number of years into the future.

Event three was the proposal for the creation of a Eurobond facility, which is the right decision for managing the financial stress existing on the continent of Europe. It took years for the member nations to finally arrive at this necessary solution. Implementation will take months, but it will likely occur.

Event four was the successful navigation of the Chinese government to reduce its national growth to less than eight percent from more than ten percent while keeping the system operating.

All of these "events" were significant unknowns at the time I began writing this book in early 2013. Those unknowns are now largely known with reasonably predictable outcomes, all of which will likely produce, over time, a more stable global environment. This creates an opportunity to begin the process of changing the financial architecture in a slow, slow, deliberate manner to allow economies to resume sustainable growth patterns.

My view: Just as my therapists helped me to relearn basic functions, our nation is going to relearn how to operate in this newly developing world.

What to watch for: slow-slow-think-small incremental progress, starting in the United States and gradually working throughout the global marketplace. Progress must be steady and painstaking if we are to transition to sustainable growth. For those of you reading this who are clients, watch for portfolio adjustments to begin occurring now and to be consistently transitioned over the coming months and quarters. Ultimately—and the process could take quarters, not weeks—we will experience greater inflation and a return to normal interest rates.

The financial adviser in me reviews the current capital sitting on the sidelines of the American financial system; it is waiting as if in suspended animation. The $2.7 trillion in money-market mutual funds added to the cash sitting in the US banking system, plus the healthy balance sheets of corporate America, is surplus and liquid, poised to move if properly motivated. The decision of policy makers to leave interest rates at zero all the way through the next calendar year also adds to the mix. My view here is the economy will signal a rise in interest rates long before the two years elapse. It's nice to understand that when this next megatrend is untracked, it won't need a government stimulus or bailout (or bail in, depending upon your point of view). The capital is already in place to fund expansion.

The entrepreneur in me views the 23 million Americans—probably more—unable to secure the right job as idle capacity waiting to be engaged.

The final piece to this is the breathtaking accelerator of integrative technology. During the "lost decade," Moore's law was not suspended. The computer industry has continued its productivity improvements. When we decommission our computers every three years, we budget $100,000 to upgrade our systems to keep in stride with Wall Street. (We have a direct connection to the exchanges, which requires we have state-of-the-art systems.) Last year was our year to execute the transition. The cost was a simple $15,000 with a management decision to opt for cloud computing services at a small monthly rate. We now have the capacity to grow our enterprise 30 percent without adding to our existing expenses. Productivity indeed! If we are any indicator, and I believe we are, the big advantage goes to the small and mid-sized organizations.

Job generation is a verb. This coming economy will create jobs, lots of them. People will still need to compete for the best of them, but my guess is there will be plenty to go around. Twenty-three million—plenty? Who knows. Job generation is also a noun. It's like the moniker the Greatest Generation for those who lived through the Depression and fought World War II. New Dealers, baby boomers, generation Xers, Yers or Zers, millennials—why couldn't the next cohort be labeled the job generation?

> "New Dealers, baby boomers, generation Xers, Yers or Zers, millennials—why couldn't the next cohort be labeled the job generation?"

The job generation. Hmm. I kinda like the sound of that ... might make a good book title.

Understanding the six elements of an entrepreneurial mind is a trigger point to igniting this new generation. Now we've fully covered the six major elements of an entrepreneurial mind. Now you have an understanding of how weird, how unusual—unique might be a better word—entrepreneurs are and how they're wired and how they think.

Because of these insights, the material in this book is required reading—as a textbook for my class, Entrepreneurial Leadership. Some students use this material to form start-up entrepreneurial businesses. Other students use this material as they interview with entrepreneurial organizations to guide them in distinguishing themselves from the noisy crowd of competitive jobseekers. What they're looking for is the right job. They use the material in this book to demonstrate that they understand what it's like to be an entrepreneur and to work in an entrepreneurial business. It helps them get to the right job, not just the next job. Maybe it helps them develop skills they can use to create an entire career. Maybe it can help them discover their calling, answering questions such as what am I supposed to do? What am I really good at? What do I really enjoy doing? And maybe the answers will apply to an entrepreneurial business.

People who attend my speaking engagements will be able to purchase this book. Unsecured workers will get an inside view of the way entrepreneurs are wired and how they think. This book should resonate deeply with entrepreneurs. It can initiate new focused thinking and invigorate a dull business or maybe start something new, maybe jump-start a business that somehow has just gone into being in the doldrums. It might also allow you to better understand what you must look for in new hires who will be complementary to your business vision and help your business grow.

> "Maybe it can help them discover their calling, answering questions such as what am I supposed to do? What am I really good at? What do I really enjoy doing? And maybe the answers will apply to an entrepreneurial business."

At Destiny Capital we wrote the book because we're a different kind of consulting firm. We consult from what I like to call "alley smarts," though some might use the phrase street smarts. Certainly, we are well steeped in academic achievements. Multiple master's degrees and diplomas adorn the walls of our offices. We have almost four decades of experience in a continuing financial advisory practice.

> It's a new improved bulletin board with a laser beam focus on entrepreneurs and the people who want to work in the new and creative companies those entrepreneurs are developing.

We work from Main Street to Wall Street, but there's another level that's deeper, more solid. It comes from the pioneer mountain-men, trapper/trader DNA in my blood. It's where Main Street really gets down to basics and gets business done, not necessarily as in the shining skyscrapers of Manhattan, nor even as in the clean shop fronts of Main Street, but as in understanding the nitty-gritty of the reality of business as it works hard in the alleys. That's what this book reveals.

Now, the minute this book came off the printing press and the electronic version entered the digital world, it was finished. Its linear voyage was done. It had reached its destination. But we're not a linear world; we're a circular world. So the book's content lives on in an electronic format on a website that's dedicated to entrepreneurial leaders who want to continue to learn and teach others.

The website is also designed for unsecured workers who want to learn and teach, and who can do so by participating in the forums.

I'm the conductor, with baton in hand, coordinating both elements, the entrepreneurial businesses and the workers who want to gravitate to them. This electronic community is where you can meet and understand one another. It's also a place where you'll be able to find one another in the deluge that is the marketplace today. It's a new improved bulletin board with a laser beam focus on entrepreneurs and the people who want to work in the new and creative companies those entrepreneurs are developing.

> **"In the United States of America, we should be able to find a job for everybody, every living person, every able-bodied productive person who wants one. This book is a start."**

Unless I'm mistaken, I think the next explosion, the next big move in American business is going to be small- and medium-sized entrepreneurial companies. That's where the great jobs are going to be. This book, this work, the website, the speaking engagements, the teaching that I'm doing at the university—all of that is dedicated to harnessing this next move for America.

In a country our size, it's not a good thing that 23 million or more of us can't find the right job. In the United States of America, we should be able to find a job for everybody, every living person, every able-bodied productive person who wants one. This book is a start. This is my place. I can do something about that problem. This is my effort. The end of this book is not the end of this book. The end of this book is inviting you to an ongoing conversation.

My company's website EMPOWERIUM.com (see the contact page for full connectivity) continues this work of job generation. It features a blog, to which an interactive community of entrepreneurial business owners contribute, writing about their businesses and their opportunities. These are companies that employ my consulting service, or organizations that contacted my company as a result of a conference presentation. It is a place where my students at the University of Denver write about their needs as future workers. The purpose of this electronic community is to help these two groups of people understand one another for their mutual benefit. Think of this as a community matching job seekers with those having opportunities for the right workers. This site and the blog also support the speaking and consulting aspects of our work. While I teach entrepreneurial leadership at a university, I also speak and teach in the business community. All of that activity is coordinated through this site. Key in the following URL to visit.

http://www.empowerium.com/blog/

At this point I want to thank you, the reader. If you made it this far, I want to thank you for your time, and for taking the opportunity to learn with me. However, if you get to the end of the book and you feel that it was a waste of your time, get in touch with us. Send a message on our website and we'll refund you the price of the book.

We want you to feel your time and money spent with us was worthwhile. Your time as an entrepreneur, and as a job seeker is valuable and worthy of respect. That's one of the unique characteristics of my own financial advisory firm. If clients are not satisfied with the work that we have done for them, we refund their fees. And so it is for you as a reader of this book.

Why? It's a character thing. It's a separator. We do it because it's a quality measure. It keeps us on our toes. So in this case, if you read all the way to the end of this book and think, "This really didn't resonate with me. I didn't get my money's worth," send us your address and contact information along with your proof of purchase and we'll mail you a check.

On the other hand, if there were parts of this book that made you go "Hmm," if there were parts of this book that triggered something in you, join the entrepreneurial leaders. Go to our website **http://www. empowerium.com** and check us out. Hang around for a bit. Join the community. Become part of something that's continuing to grow and continuing to make a difference.

All of this harkens back to why I wrote this book, some of which I detailed in the introduction.

As you remember in the introduction, I spoke about the commencement speech at my alma mater in June 2012. The commencement speaker essentially said that his generation inherited a paradise from his fathers and his forefathers—his ancestors. Over the 40-year period of his working life, his generation turned it into a mess. He said, "You guys are in for a horrific environment as new graduates. You're inheriting a broken, debt-ridden, bankrupt system, and we broke it. I apologize to you, but it's your job to fix it."

When he said, "It's your job to fix it" to the new graduates of my university, there was something that exploded in the middle of my guts, and I said, "Not on my watch. It's not the responsibility of newly graduated students to fix the problem." I'm 57 years old. I inherited a paradise, just as this man did. What the commencement speaker said was accurate, but it's my job to do what I can to fix it.

That's why I wrote the book, it's why we have the electronic community going, and it's why I volunteered to teach at University of Denver (they loved my concepts and ideas so much, they actually hired me as an adjunct. I know—go figure) to be able to create new businesses that create new jobs and have graduate students be able to find the right job.

As I've spent time over the last six months field testing this material in the lead up to writing this book, I've discovered that there are a lot of entrepreneurial businesses that need their pencils sharpened. They need to get better at what they do. I can help. This book will help them. There are a whole bunch of unsecured workers and unfulfilled workers who are misplaced and are not in the right jobs. This book will help them, and it will help you, too.

> "There are a whole bunch of unsecured workers and unfulfilled workers who are misplaced and are not in the right jobs. This book will help them, and it will help you, too."

I wrote this book for them, and the electronic community is specifically designed to give them methods and tools that will help them create separation in a competitive marketplace. That's my contribution to fixing the problem. I'm not going to leave that to the next generation. That's my job. I'm in my last third of life and I'm going to make my last third count for something.

At that commencement address, which I attended with my wife—we both spend a lot of time volunteering and mentoring students—many of those sitting in the auditorium were my students. I really have a great respect for the commencement speaker. He built an empire in the newspaper business, but he's now watching the newspaper business dissolve right underneath him. He basically said, "Hey, this is a mess, but it's your job to fix it. Get right to it." It left the students angry and disillusioned. We got hit with a tidal wave of negative emotion over that. There was a big part of me that said, "Wait a minute. I can do something about that."

> "The future is in your hands; it is for you to keep America working long into the decades ahead."

I can't solve the whole problem, but I've learned a thing or two over 37 years that specifically addresses a monster need in the marketplace now, both for companies and for the people who want to work in them, especially small, entrepreneurial companies. What I've learned you've seen in the stories and anecdotes I've told. I've picked anecdotes from totally different industries because what I'm talking about applies universally. It works for manufacturing, it works for distribution and sales, it works for technology, and it works for service businesses. There isn't any business where this stuff doesn't fit. I have given many examples in this book, from woodworking to washing machines, but no matter the business, the lessons are the same. And they can work for you, whether you are an entrepreneur or a job seeker. It is all about your own laser focus and bringing your skills to the market place.

Now, here's a little more about my class at the Daniels College of Business at the University of Denver, one of this country's most renowned business schools. What do I love doing? I love standing in front of a new generation, and I want to teach them about how to get great jobs. I want to teach them how to create wonderful companies. The future is in your hands; it is for you to keep America working long into the decades ahead.

Thanks for joining me. You can find the curriculum ahead.

DANIELS COLLEGE OF BUSINESS

MANAGEMENT DEPARTMENT

TITLE: Entrepreneurial Leadership (EL)

SUBTITLE: CREATING COMPANIES THAT WORK WHILE LEARNING HOW TO WORK WITHIN CREATIVE COMPANIES.

COURSE OBJECTIVES:

1. Learn how companies are formed.

2. Understand how EL organizations work in real-life circumstances.

3. Personal discovery if entrepreneurship is within the make-up of each student.

4. Personal discovery of how to "fit" into any organization that is entrepreneurial. Learning the specifics of how to relate to entrepreneurial organizations as a method of becoming the newest employee to work within the company.

5. Learning how to scout out opportunities within entrepreneurial organizations which are not even listed on internal electronic communications or external job postings.

6. Demonstration through weekly projects (six total) to submit in writing and present in class. Each unit represents part of a cumulative building block to creating a new company.

7. Experience 360 degree performance evaluations.

8. Give 360 degree performance evaluations.

9. Develop interpersonal leadership skills working cross-culturally in strategic work teams.

10. Make a presentation to birth a real live company using the coursework materials.

11. Weekly class discussions to evaluate the veracity of business planning elements presented each week.

REQUIRED COURSE MATERIALS:

Text book: *Job Generation* by Steven R . Musick

Blog posts from the website www.Empowerium.com, an online community designed to have ongoing conversations between EL organizations and the people wanting to secure the right jobs within them.

Specific articles from prior issues of *Entrepreneur* magazine selected by the professor.

PHILOSOPHY AND PEDAGOGY:

Every student is the fee paying customer.

Engagement is governed by the principles of cooperation requiring mutual dedication to achieve:

Force to perform is met with equal assistance to produce. A student's consistency and diligence of force to perform behavior will be met with equal assistance to produce from the professor and panel members.

The class will be randomly divided into strategic work groups at the first class. These groups will work collectively and collaboratively during the entire course.

The course will have elements of lecture, interactive discussions: student to student, group to group, student and group to professor. There will also be an element of student groups presenting and having dialog with existing and former entrepreneurs and professionals in the investment/fund raising community of Denver.

Each week each group will be making presentations on each of the six elements of EL.

The final for the course will be a 20-minute complete presentation on a complete business plan using all six elements of the course to the class and to a panel comprised of the professor, other Daniels professors, current and former entrepreneurs, investor groups and the other groups.

GRADING SCALE WILL BE STANDARD ONE USED THROUGHOUT DANIELS

GRADING METHODOLOGY:

1. Attendance—10 percent

2. Weekly element presentations—18 percent; 9 percent by peers (1.5 percent per element) + 9 percent by professor (also 1.5 percent per element.) Each group will be evaluated and reviewed by every other group and by the professor every other week.

3. Written presentations—12 percent. Written presentations submitted for each element and integrated into all previous elements in a comprehensive cumulative manner. Remember the students are building real companies.

4. Final presentation—20 percent

    a. 5 percent from the panel of professors.

    b. 5 percent from the student groups.

    c. 5 percent entrepreneurial businesses.

    d. 5 percent investor groups.

5. Final presentation—40 percent by the professor.

ULTIMATE RESULTS:

The company(s) with the best comprehensive presentations demonstrating veracity and viability will be mentored into existence by the professor and funded by the investors on the panel—0 percent grade; 100 percent purpose of education.

Each student in the class will at their request receive extensive job interview coaching by the professor, designed to assist the student secure the right job.

CONTINUOUS FEEDBACK ON COURSE REQUIREMENTS PROVIDED DURING THE ENTIRE 10 WEEKS

PROFESSOR IS AVAILABLE 24/7 FOR DIALOG THROUGH EMPOWERIUM.COM

About Daniels College of Business

For this chapter of the book I could have had a PR student/intern at Daniels rifle through web material and brochures lifting out tasty nuggets of information that would wow readers. I encourage you to do an online search of Daniels College at the University of Denver and read all about it at your leisure.

Why Daniels?

I could have connected with the University of Colorado or Colorado State University or even any one of the community colleges within my city. Frankly, at any of them it would have been easier to become an adjunct professor than at Daniels. There is an unwritten rule about not employing alumni, especially recent, midcareer graduate students (remember, my master's degree in global studies (MGS) with an emphasis on international economics was earned at the University of Denver in 2006.) But, I took road less travelled, hoping to make all the difference. (Apologies to Robert Frost.)

Remember also that I am a native of Colorado, second generation back to 1927. My father graduated from the University of Denver, as did my son Jarrod in 2009. Remember also my ancestors were trappers, traders, and mountain men. This university was started in 1864, about the time my grandfather's grandfather came out of the mountains to settle in homestead sections of Colorado that are now within the city limits of Denver. I have this visceral drive to continue on in the Musick tradition, reaching back into history to propel me into the future. I have roots within the University of Denver. Over the ten years my wife, Elaine, and I have been mentoring students here, there has been a deep sense of belonging to something greater than ourselves. Investing in the next generation in this location is emotionally—yes, even spiritually—rewarding. A private university, dedicated to the public good. Hmm—resonates all the way into my soul to be on campus connecting with the next generation, the next JOB GENERATION.

Is there such a place in your life? Is there a place where your roots and your ancestors feed you, encourage you forward into the future and a hope for the country to come?

Think about it. I believe you can find it.

APPENDIX

Directional Dozen: How We Work As One
Three Foundation Essentials

Mission

Vision

Core Values

Mission: Managing family wealth for generations

Vision: To be a company that courageously cares for people

Core Values:

1. Integrity assured through transparency;
   no hidden conflicts of interest;

2. Patience because haste brings poverty;

3. Dedication through cooperative effort; clients
   do their part (providing time and information);
   we do our part to serve them.

The Necessary Nine

Just as scaffolding and the girding supported the reconstruction of the Statue of Liberty, so does the Necessary Nine support our mission, vision, and core values:

9. Organizational development

8. Team building

7. Leadership

6. Teaching gifts

5. Management

4. Experience

3. Education and training

2. Talent

1. Effort

Components 1 and 2 are both components of raw material required to be part of the Destiny team.

1. **Effort:** making a personal decision to desire a positive outcome

2. **Talent:** ability and aptitude, capacity to learn new things, and God-given fundamental foundation ability

Components 3 and 4 are both elements of the refinery process for components 1 and 2.

3. **Education:** the continuous acquisition of knowledge through formal courses and practical experimentation for use in real life; training: the continuous, hands-on, interactive, specific information and coaching to improve performance in real life;

4. **Experience:** the combination of training and education multiplied by (not simply added to) application in real life.

The *continuous* process of refining component 1 (effort) and component 2 (talent) through the use of components 3 (education and training) and 4 (experience) enables every team member the opportunity to obtain exceptional career opportunities.

5. **Management:** the daily process of focusing all the aspects of our firm: the three foundational essentials combine with the first four of The Necessary Nine components, to create an environment that facilitates individual growth *and* team building.

6. **Teaching gifts:** The ability to assist people to combine: 1 (effort) and 2 (talent) with 3 (education and training) and 4 (experience) to produce quality results at an accelerated rate.

It is our heartfelt desire to do ourselves what we expect of all our team members:

Seven Principles of Leadership

1. All people should be fully equipped and ready to serve every day.

2. We take care of our team members *and* their families by 1) including all family members on our regular special events, and 2) being truly interested in more than *just* business productivity!

3. We encourage and model loyalty to one another.

4. We teach by example in thought, word, and deed.

5. We *never* pass by a mistake. We view it as an opportunity for learning.

6. We do what is *right. Always!*

7. We communicate openly, directly, honestly, and freely with each other and management.

8. **We build teams.** We have the ability and the desire to synergize with coworkers for the benefit of our clients and, as a result, benefit ourselves—*in that order.* No Lone Rangers exist in our firm. There will *never* be room for them in the future.

9. **We foster organizational development.** We strive to become an organization that has the ability to reach high to grasp the destiny that has been set before us, to make a positive difference in every challenge

we encounter together, and to improve the financial health of each client we are privileged to serve.

The reconstruction of the Statue of Liberty was ultimately completed. The supportive structures were removed to reveal the refurbished work. We see that the work of management, however, is never done. We all are perpetually under construction and therefore our enterprise, unlike the real Statue of Liberty, will forever have the scaffolding and girding of The Necessary Nine to support the three foundational essentials of mission, vision, and core values.

The three foundational essentials that bring forth liberty, supported by the scaffolding and girding of the management structure for continuous improvements under construction—this is the management style of Destiny Capital

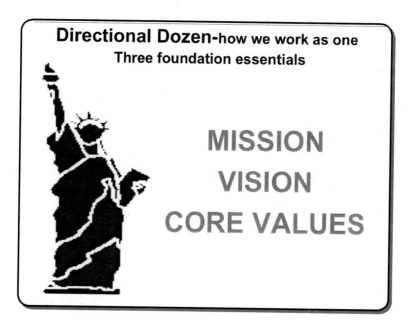

Directional Dozen-how we work as one
Three foundation essentials

MISSION:
Managing family wealth for generations.

Directional Dozen-how we work as one
Three foundation essentials

VISION:
To be a company that courageously cares for people

Directional Dozen-how we work as one
Three foundation essentials

CORE VALUES:

Integrity assured through transparency no hidden conflicts of interest.

Directional Dozen-how we work as one
Three foundation essentials

CORE VALUES:

Patience because haste bring poverty

Directional Dozen-how we work as one
Three foundation essentials

CORE VALUES:

Dedication through cooperative effort- clients do their part (providing time and information) we do our part to serve them.

Directional Dozen-how we work as one

THE NECESSARY NINE

As the scaffolding and the girding supported the reconstruction of the statue of liberty so does **THE NECESSARY NINE** support our mission, vision, and core values.

Directional Dozen-how we work as one
THE NECESSARY NINE

9. Organizational development

8. Team building

7. Leadership

6. Teaching gifts

5. Management

4. Experience

3. Education & Training

2. Talent

1. Effort

Directional Dozen-how we work as one
THE NECESSARY NINE

9. Organizational development

8. Team building

7. Leadership

6. Teaching gifts

5. Management

4. Experience

3. Education & Training

2. Talent

1. Effort

THE NECESSARY NINE

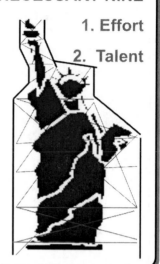

1. Effort
2. Talent

1 and 2 are both components of raw material required to be part of the DESTINY team.

Effort- making a personal decision to desire a positive outcome.

Talent- ability and aptitude, capacity to learn new things, and God given fundamental foundation ability.

Directional Dozen-how we work as one
THE NECESSARY NINE

9. Organizational development
8. Team building
7. Leadership
6. Teaching gifts
5. Management
4. **Experience**
3. **Education & Training**
2. **Talent**
1. **Effort**

THE NECESSARY NINE

3 and 4 are both elements of the refinery process for 1 and 2.

Education-the *continuous* acquisition of knowledge through formal courses and practical experimentation for use in *real life*. **Training**-the *continuous* hands on interactive specific information and coaching to improve performance in *real life*.

Experience-the combination of training and education *multiplied by* (not simply added to) application in *real life*.

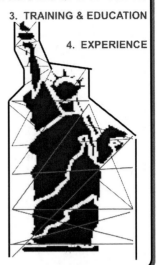

3. TRAINING & EDUCATION

4. EXPERIENCE

Directional Dozen-how we work as one
THE NECESSARY NINE

9. Organizational development

8. Team building

7. Leadership

6. Teaching gifts

5. Management

4. Experience

3. Education & Training

2. Talent

1. Effort

THE NECESSARY NINE

The *continuous* process of refining 1 effort and 2 talent through the use of 3 education & training and 4 experience to enable every team member the opportunity to obtain exceptional career opportunities.

5. management

Management- is the daily process of focusing all the aspects of our firm, the 3 foundation essentials with the first 4 of necessary nine, to create an environment that produces a culture which facilitates individual growth *and* team building.

Directional Dozen-how we work as one
THE NECESSARY NINE

9. Organizational development

8. Team building

7. Leadership

6. Teaching gifts

5. Management

4. Experience

3. Education & Training

2. Talent

1. Effort

THE NECESSARY NINE

6. teaching gifts

Teaching gifts-The ability to assist people to combine: **1** effort and **2** talent with **3** education & training and **4** experience to produce quality results at an accelerated rate.

Directional Dozen-how we work as one

THE NECESSARY NINE

9. Organizational development

8. Team building

7. **Leadership**

6. **Teaching gifts**

5. **Management**

4. **Experience**

3. **Education & Training**

2. **Talent**

1. **Effort**

THE NECESSARY NINE

It is our heartfelt determined desire to do personally what we expect of all team members of our firm.

7. leadership

7 principles of leadership

1. All people should be fully equipped ready to serve every day.

2. Take care of our team members _and_ their families by: 1)including all family members on our regular special events. And 2) being truly interested in more than _just_ business productivity!

3. Encourage and model loyalty to one another.

4. Teach by example in thought word and deed

5. _Never_ pass by a mistake. View it as an opportunity for learning.

6. Do what is _right !!!! Always!!!!_

7. Communicate openly, directly, honestly and freely toward each other and toward management.

Directional Dozen-how we work as one
THE NECESSARY NINE

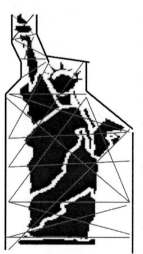

9. Organizational development

8. **Team building**

7. **Leadership**

6. **Teaching gifts**

5. **Management**

4. **Experience**

3. **Education & Training**

2. **Talent**

1. **Effort**

THE NECESSARY NINE

8. Team building

     The ability and the desire to synergize with coworkers for the benefit of our clients _and_ as a result benefit ourselves....

        ......In that order!!!!!

     There exists now no Lone rangers in our firm. There will _never_ be room for them in the future.

Directional Dozen-how we work as one

THE NECESSARY NINE

9. **Organizational development**

8. **Team building**

7. **Leadership**

6. **Teaching gifts**

5. **Management**

4. **Experience**

3. **Education & Training**

2. **Talent**

1. **Effort**

THE NECESSARY NINE

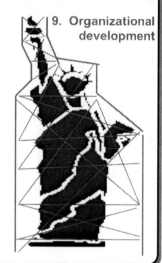

9. Organizational development

To strive to become an organization that has the ability to reach high to grasp for the **DESTINY** that has been set before us. To make a positive difference in every challenge we encounter together. To make for a better existence for each client we are privileged to serve.

Directional Dozen-how we work as one

THE NECESSARY NINE

9. Organizational development

8. Team building

7. Leadership

6. Teaching gifts

5. Management

4. Experience

3. Education & Training

2. Talent

1. Effort

Directional Dozen- How we work as one

The reconstruction of the Statue of Liberty was ultimately completed. The supportive structures removed to reveal the refurbished work. We see that the work of management however, is *never* done. We all are perpetually under construction and therefore our enterprise, unlike the real Statue of Liberty, will forever have the scaffolding and girding of **THE NECESSARY NINE** to support the three foundation essentials of mission, vision, and core values.

Directional Dozen-how we work as one

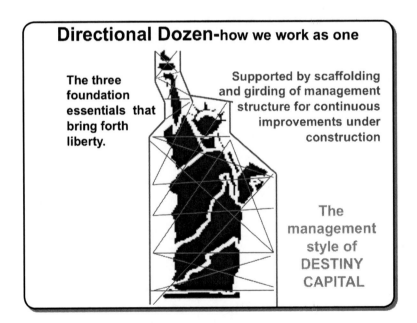

The three foundation essentials that bring forth liberty.

Supported by scaffolding and girding of management structure for continuous improvements under construction

The management style of DESTINY CAPITAL

This is a copy of our employee orientation manual. It is in a PowerPoint format and readily downloadable. Contact us at EMPOWERIUM.com and we will send it to you. Yes, it's free!

Steven R. Musick, MSM, MSFS, MGS

That academic alphabet soup represents three master's degrees: MSM is a management degree from The American College, completed in 1995. MSFS is a degree in financial services, completed in 2001, and MGS is a degree in global studies, completed in 2006 at the University of Denver, where Steve teaches today.

In 1977, as an honorably discharged, disabled military veteran, Steve started a financial advisory practice. His service-disabled status made him virtually unemployable. Using $8,000 from his own savings, he started an entrepreneurial enterprise.

That business is Destiny Capital, and it manages over $175 million of assets for clients. Steve's entire entrepreneurial spirit is in his DNA. His ancestors were trappers, traders, and mountain men. The novel *Centennial* by James Michener describes Steve's character accurately.

The year 2003 brought a mentoring dynamic to his life. He and his wife, Elaine, began working with college students at the University of Denver. Together, the husband and wife entrepreneurial team helped students build a bridge from the academic world of school to the commercial world of work.

That "work" expanded and become formal in 2006 with the creation of the Destiny Capital fund for students. It operates on the principal of compound giving—that is, the giving of time and of talent along with the treasure of money to bring about exponential results.

In 2013 the university accepted Steve's application to become an adjunct professor, teaching entrepreneurial leadership at the Daniel's College of Business. The book you are holding is required reading for the course.

Academic training in management, economics, and finance, combined with an entrepreneurial DNA spirit, added to a multigenerational, successful business—that's Steve Musick.

But those are not the reasons to read the book or select him as a speaker or even hire him as a consultant. This has been simply the first two-thirds of his life. The final one-third is about jobs. Securing the right job eludes many while building the right workforce is a challenge to many entrepreneurial organizations. Steve has stepped in to solve this problem by creating a bridge.

That bridge catalyzes job generation, which Steve does through teaching, lectures, and speaking, through an electronic community, and through business-to-business consulting. This is the best use of his collection of life's experiences. And it's his final one-third of life dedication. It's what he'll be doing for the rest of his life.

What's in the Musick Library?

The Musick library is divided into sections and further segmented by author.

The Business Section

Stephen Covey:
> *7 Habits of Highly Successful People*
> *The 8th Habit*
> *Everyday Greatness*
> *Principled Centered Leadership*

Thomas L. Friedman
> *The World Is Flat*
> *Hot, Flat, and Crowded*
> *That Used to Be Us*

Peters and Waterman
> *In Search of Excellence*

Max Depree
> *Leadership Is an Art*

Kouzes and Posner
> *Leadership Challenge*
> *The Truth about Leadership*

Jim Collins
> *Good to Great*

Malcolm Gladwell
> *Tipping Point*
> *Blink*
> *What the Dog Saw*
> *Outliers*

Bakke
> *Joy at Work*

Brafman and Beckstrom
> *The Starfish and the Spider*

Jennifer James
> *Thinking in the Future Tense*

Alan Greenspan
> *The Age of Turbulence*

Leif Edvinsson and Michael Malone
> *Intellectual Capital*

Tony Dungy
> *The Mentor Leader*

Gary Becker
> *The Economics of Life*

McNair Wilson
> *Hatch*

Lee Child
> *the entire Jack Reacher series, all 17 books to remind me to be free, carefree, principled, and a defender of what is right*

Contact

The electronic community connected
to this book can be found at:

Empowerium.com

The author can be reached at:

Steven R. Musick
Destiny Capital Corporation
13922 Denver West Pkwy. #150
Golden, Colorado 80401
phone 303.277.9977
fax 303.277.9977

If you Google **Steven R. Musick**, the first link is his Linked In page.

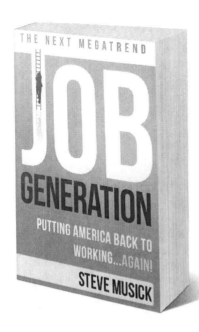

How can you use this book?

MOTIVATE

EDUCATE

THANK

INSPIRE

PROMOTE

CONNECT

Why have a custom version of *Job Generation*?

- Build personal bonds with customers, prospects, employees, donors, and key constituencies
- Develop a long-lasting reminder of your event, milestone, or celebration
- Provide a keepsake that inspires change in behavior and change in lives
- Deliver the ultimate "thank you" gift that remains on coffee tables and bookshelves
- Generate the "wow" factor

Books are thoughtful gifts that provide a genuine sentiment that other promotional items cannot express. They promote employee discussions and interaction, reinforce an event's meaning or location, and they make a lasting impression. Use your book to say "Thank You" and show people that you care.

Job Generation is available in bulk quantities and in customized versions at special discounts for corporate, institutional, and educational purposes. To learn more please contact our Special Sales team at:

1.866.775.1696 • sales@advantageww.com • www.AdvantageSpecialSales.com

CPSIA information can be obtained at www.ICGtesting.com
Printed in the USA
LVOW06s1338120713

342647LV00006B/83/P